Do less...

of the corporate silliness.

Ignore more of the noise and senseless stuff that comes your way.

You deserve better.

You deserve to spend more of your time and talent on what truly matters.

The Simplicity Survival Handbook

First Indian Edition 2009

VIVA BOOKS PRIVATE LIMITED

- 4737/23 Ansari Road, Daryaganj, New Delhi 110 002
  E-mail: vivadelhi@vivagroupindia.net, Tel. 42242200
- 76, Service Industries, Shirvane, Sector 1, Nerul, Navi Mumbai 400 706
  E-mail: vivamumbai@vivagroupindia.net, Tel. 27721273, 27721274
- Jamals Fazal Chambers, 26 Greams Road, Chennai 600 006
  E-mail: vivachennai@vivagroupindia.net, Tel. 28290304, 28294241
- B-103, Jindal Towers, 21/1A/3 Darga Road, Kolkata 700 017
  E-mail: vivakolkata@vivagroupindia.net, Tel. 22836381, 22816713
- 7, Sovereign Park Apartments, 56-58, K. R. Road, Basavanagudi, Bangalore 560 004
  E-mail: vivabangalore@vivagroupindia.net, Tel. 26607409, 26607410
- 101-102 Mughal Marc Apartments, 3-4-637 to 641, Narayanguda, Hyderabad 500 029
  E-mail: vivahyderabad@vivagroupindia.net, Tel. 27564481, 27564482
- First Floor, Beevi Towers, SRM Road, Kaloor, Kochi 682 018, Kerala
  E-mail: vivakochi@vivagroupindia.net, Tel: 0484-2403055, 2403056
- H. No. 12, P. B. Road, Reha Basti, Near Arya Hospital, Guwahati 781 008
  E-mail: vivaguwahati@vivagroupindia.net, Tel: 0361-2735624

www.vivagroupindia.com

Published by arrangement with

Perseus Books
A member of the Perseus Books LLC
Eleven Cambridge Centre
Cambridge MA 02142
USA

ISBN-10: 81-7649-879-3
ISBN-13: 978-81-7649-879-1

Published by Vinod Vasishtha for Viva Books Private Limited, 4737/23, Ansari Road, Daryaganj, New Delhi - 110 002.

Printed and bound by Anand Sons, Delhi - 110 092.

The Simplicity Survival Handbook

32 WAYS TO DO LESS AND ACCOMPLISH MORE

Bill Jensen

Viva Books

New Delhi | Mumbai | Chennai | Kolkata | Bangalore | Hyderabad | Kochi | Guwahati

The Simplicity Survival Handbook: 32 Ways to Do Less and Accomplish More

Choose Your Own Adventure

Radical simplicity: Read only what you need and ignore the rest

- Create your own 50-page book
- Select only three to four chapters
- Tear out the Do-Less Toolkit

Contents

Section 2: Career Milestones

For those who want a...

Cut-to-the-Chase Introduction

You could write a more scathing, bold, and brilliant introduction than me — because you've lived through every problem I've studied, and have the skid marks on your back to prove it.

All you need are the tools.

Fast.

And all you want are the stripped-down to-do's.

OK…

1. Go to the Do-Less Toolkit on page 265
2. Rip out those 15 pages, and toss the rest of this book
3. Use the tools. Follow the Laws•O•Less

The Toolkit reduces everything in the book to summary checklists. Of course, you'll miss out on BlahBlahBlah — (fill in with whatever authors say about every word they write being important) — but you'll still get a huge return on whatever you paid for this book.

for more ⇨

For those who want a...

Tour Guide Introduction

Why You're Reading This Book

There's too much silliness, noise, and crap coming at you, and you want to find the shut-off valve. You want to do less, and accomplish more — making more of a difference, and working only on what truly matters. Right?

Why I Wrote This Book

I've been studying work complexity for more than a decade. (See below: Search for a Simpler Way.) From that research, I've designed a book of workarounds and shut-off valves — ways to get around or stop the senseless stuff that comes at you every day.

The tools in this book work. They've been field-tested by people just like you, so I know that you can *use* most every idea to immediately create simpler workdays for yourself.

But I also hope you will *feel* something after reading these pages....

If you are an employee, or a mid-manager, or free agent:

- You don't have to be a victim of corporate crap, nor do you have to perpetuate it.
- There are ways you can do something about it — (surprise!) — *without* jeopardizing your job.
- You have a lot more control over your workload than you think you do.

If you are a senior executive...Speaking the truth to power:

You are gonna love some of the chapters in this book!
They will truly help you drive clarity and focus throughout your organization.
Other chapters, frankly, you may hate.
Don't worry. I'm not an anarchist.
This isn't a manual for overthrowing your company.
I'm merely telling you the truth about behaviors I have seen in your organization. Your employees won't tell you that they're already doing workarounds on stuff that you think are important, but they think are silly, wasteful, and an ineffective use of their time and talents.
So I will.
From there, it's up to you.
Will you banish this book, and create policies to stop the workarounds? Or will you use this as a handbook to change the conversation about leadership, communication, productivity, workflow, efficiency, and more?

How to Use This Handbook

Warning: Do not read cover-to-cover

This is really just a 50-page book: easy enough to read on a plane ride, and then put to immediate use. To get it there, I need your help:

1. **Pick (only!) the three or four chapters** that scream at you:
   "Yesssss! This is the stupid stuff I've been dying to deal with!"

2. **Follow the steps in each chapter**
   (If you want more, read *why* the steps work. Not required, but highly recommended.)

3. **Rip out the Do-Less Toolkit pages** at the back of the book
   Tack 'em up wherever you'll see them every day. Be one with those pages. Do less.

This is a Book About Respect

Respecting yourself more:

Doing less stuff that really doesn't matter, and treating the limited time you have as more precious.

Respecting others more:

Recognizing that every communication you send, every meeting you conduct, and every to-do you assign to others uses a portion of someone else's life.

•

Throat-Clearing Disclaimer:

Doing less and laziness are not the same thing

This is not a guide to laziness.

On every page you will find accountabilities that you own, and cannot shirk. The second half of the subtitle is ...*Accomplish More.* This isn't a license to tell your boss to stick it just because he doesn't get it. This isn't a goof-off manual. This is a book about doing less stupid stuff so you can make more of a difference. And work only on what truly matters. That's what you said you wanted, right?

•

The Search for a Simpler Way

In 1992, I began an ongoing research project, *The Search for a Simpler Way*. We started with 2,500 people in 460 companies. The study has now grown to over 1,000 companies, and we have surveyed, interviewed, or focus grouped more than 350,000 individuals around the globe.

Early on, we found that most work complexity actually originates from *within* your own company. The biggest day-to-day problems, complexities, frustrations, and confusion are *not* caused by outside forces (like the economy or competition), but instead come from how leaders, managers, and employees react to those forces — making the next steps hard instead of easy, muddied and unfocused instead of clear, complicated instead of simple.

Since '92, my mission has been to make it easier for people to get stuff done. My conversations with people like you have turned me into a passionate simpleton, a plain-spoken advocate of common sense, a bold defender of your time and attention, and an outspoken gadfly against corporate stupidity and waste.

•

The Art and Science of Less•O•Meters

Over a six-month period, a panel of more than 260 people evaluated, challenged, changed, and tried every how-to in this book. (Many of the panelists wish to remain anonymous. Their bosses must never know that they helped create workarounds for corporate foolishness.)

To help you with each how-to, I created Less•O•Meters: ranking the amount of courage required and difficulty of implementation. Also, the yield you might expect from trying these ideas. We used a 1–10 scale, 1 = lowest, 10 = highest.

Panelist feedback was extremely polarized. No one sat on the fence after seeing my initial scores. There were two camps:

- Those who worked in small companies or entrepreneurial cultures consistently said: "I'm OK with how you scored the meters. These steps aren't that difficult or take too much courage."
- Those in larger companies or top-down cultures were extremely sensitive to the politics of doing less. "You've underestimated courage by at least 2–5 notches" was typical of their feedback.

(In the spirit of compromise, the needle position on every Less•O•Meter is the average of all panelists' feedback.)

•

My big aha: Frankly — still, after decades of talk of "empowered employees" — I was blown away by how much courage it takes, in many companies, to: ignore an email; not go to a meeting; or to bypass the stupid stuff, that everybody knows is stupid, but keeps doing anyway because that's what the boss wants. Asking people to rank the courage it takes to actually do less or to say "no" was a mind-opener for me.

I already knew that simplicity is about power:

- Simplicity is the power to do less (of what *doesn't* matter).
- Simplicity is the power to do more (of what *does* matter.)

In writing this book, I discovered that — for each of us — the depth of our character, conviction, and priorities is revealed when we must choose between doing less or doing more. For many in today's workplace, the choice to do less can be an act of courage. If that's you, this is your field guide for being bold, bodacious, and brazen — while still keeping your job!

•

My Promise to You, My Faith in You

My promise to you is that *The Simplicity Survival Handbook* will take you as far as you want to go.

If all you want are a few shut-off values — cool! Use whatever works for you. Pick a couple chapters that you can put to use immediately, and ignore the rest.

But if you want to explore the depth of your own priorities, and discover new ways to respect yourself and others, I promise you'll find that and more in these pages. And I promise some of ideas will push you out of your comfort zone. Which is a good thing.

•

One of the chapters you'll read is How to Decide: Stay or Go? When seeing it in draft-form, one manager responded, "Is this realistic, in today's economy, to say: *Stay if your manager and company support your efforts. Go if they don't.* I'm afraid that this could turn people off — make them think the book is divorced from reality."

I have enough faith in you that you'll know when I'm pushing boundaries just so you can be all that you were meant to be. (I've found that most people's dreams and capabilities far exceed what they're allowed to use at work.) And enough faith that, if you discover your manager and company do not support your efforts to do less and accomplish more, you will seriously consider divorcing yourself from that reality.

Bill Jensen
bill@simplerwork.com

1

Daily Rituals

Do less...

Accomp

Communicating... Sharing... Meeting... Listening...

lish more.

1

How to

Ignore Most Corporate Communications

LESS•O•METERS

STEPS: 2

TAKEAWAY: It pays to ignore more

KEEPING SCORE: Up to 80% contains no action or consequence for ignoring it

WHY DO LESS

You get too much communication from outside your immediate team and department • You cannot pay attention to all the company-related information that you're <u>supposed</u> to • There simply is not enough time.

HOW TO DO LESS

1

Scan the communication for two bits of information:

- Action you must take
- Date or deadline for that action, within the next two to three weeks

(e.g., Your benefits enrollment forms must be returned by November 30.
Or: You're invited to attend a company-wide meeting on April 1 to learn about the new strategy.)

2

If the communication does not contain an action and a short-term date, ignore it

Hit Delete. Don't go to the meeting. Run away, as if your life depended on it.

This applies no matter who sends you this communication, and no matter where they are on the totem pole. If hitting Delete makes you feel guilty or worried that you're missing something, don't worry, the sender will most likely waste your time once again.

- There is a 69% chance you'll get this exact communication a second time.
- There is a 48% chance you'll get it a third time.
- There is a 36% chance you'll have to show up at a meeting, event, or training to review it anyway.

So why not just wait until then?

WHAT'S BEHIND DOING LESS

Early in our ongoing study, *The Search for a Simpler Way*, the Jensen Group found that most work complexity actually originates from *within* our companies. More than a decade later, certain findings, truths, and predictable behaviors keep popping up. *How We Communicate* was originally among the top three sources of work complexity. It still is. And it's getting worse.

While it's important to recognize how things have *improved* — not long ago, companies were slammed for not communicating enough —

INSIDE THE  **PROBLEM**

Company Perspective

Our research has found…

Since 1992, most companies — and their executives and support functions — have improved their ability to get their message across to employees. Most understand the need to connect everyone to the "big picture" and, overall, companies are getting a lot better at packaging corporate initiatives so they capture attention and deliver consistent messages.

Also during the past decade, many mid-size to large companies have made great improvements in giving executives media coaching, keeping them "on message," and packaging every corporate message as part of an integrated campaign. So much so, that it's becoming rare that employees will receive that message only once.

Employee Perspective

Our research has found…

Up to 80% of all the communication coming at them:

- Does not require action
- Carries no discernible consequence if they ignore it

This is why so many savvy employees use actions and deadlines as their first-line-of-defense filter.

In 2002–2003, we studied frequency of corporate communication in over 225 companies. We found that *regardless of how the employee responded* — (studying the information, asking questions, communicating it to others, or just plain ignoring it) — they still received the same communication again and again. (See previous page for repeat rates.)

This is why savvy employees ignore so much. They've realized that they can't make the clutter go away by paying attention to it.

mostly what has changed is quantity, not utility. Companies are communicating a lot more, but little of it truly helps employees make informed decisions.

We are now seeing a widening chasm between communication-savvy companies (...with greatly improved ability to capture attention, and stay "on message"...) and communication-savvy employees (...with greatly improved BS-radar, and the ability to filter out anything that's not immediately relevant and important to them).

There is both good and bad news within this communication chasm.

•

On the dark side: At the very time when we need to be learning more *from* the people who do the work, most firms are focused on perfecting how to talk *at* them.

It is disheartening to see how few companies work backwards from the needs of their employees. For example: It took one multi-national bank almost ten years to redesign their hour-long Meetings-In-A-Box for branch managers who — according to the bank's own performance management system — had less than ten minutes available to communicate what was in the box. Result: Thousands of managers struggled, blamed themselves, worked harder, grew more tense and pressured, or simply learned to ignore 83% of what they were sent — (the other 50 minutes' worth).

This is representative of what I'm finding most everywhere. Almost none of the utility and usefulness of corporate communication is driven by employee needs. It's almost entirely based upon senior executive's views of what's needed. (See Devilish Details.)

•

There is a silver lining, though! During 2002–2003, we asked over 400 people questions like:

- "Which communication do you regularly ignore?"
- "Why?"
- "What do you gain by ignoring that communication?"

• "What's in it for you?"

Employees who use a proactive strategy to reduce what they pay attention to* report an *increased* ability to work on what matters with *no significant decrease* in loyalty or understanding of company priorities. Once they understood their company's or department's priorities — (many described that understanding as just "the gist of the overall direction") — they felt comfortable ignoring a lot of company emails, notices, broadcasts — even skipping mandatory all-hands meetings. They made their decisions by selectively scanning for information that was:

1. Specifically designed to help them get their work done
2. Organized so they can make a fully-informed, and independent decision

Employees who let their manager decide what is important, what isn't, and guide them in what to pay attention to — such as interpreting what the latest edict from Corporate means to their specific department — report *greater confusion and frustration* in keeping up with change.

If you rely mainly on your manager and your company to filter noise for you, and direct you to what's important, you will pay attention to *more*, not less.

Bottom line: It pays to ignore more.

THE WAY OUT:  **EXECUTIVE COUNTER-MOVES**

If you're a senior executive, and want all employees to pay attention to what you have to say, **go to the Do-Less Toolkit, tear out the Behavioral Communication model, and hand it to your Corporate Communication team.** They need to always answer the five questions in the model. Also: See Chapter 29, How to Turn Transparency Into an Advantage.

* Including, but not limited to corporate communication

DEVILISH DETAILS

1992–1997

Only 9% of senior managers defined communication as **"organizing and delivering useful information that people need to do their work."** [1]

Exec quote: "That's management, not communication!"

Only 6% believed strategic communication included **"the design of information people could use to make decisions,"** while 89% defined it as "delivering our strategic plan."

Employee quote: "Enough with the 'why we're changing' crap. I want solid info I can use to make real decisions. Not just 'context setting.'"

2002–2003

9% (above) had only improved to **14%** [2]

The stand-out firms can be found on most any *Best Place to Work* list. But they are the exceptions, not the rule.

Interviewed/surveyed: 1. 426 2. 186

WANT MORE?

The original *Search for a Simpler Way* study findings, plus updates, can be downloaded for free at www.simplerwork.com

2

How to

Delete 75% of Your Emails

LESS•O•METERS

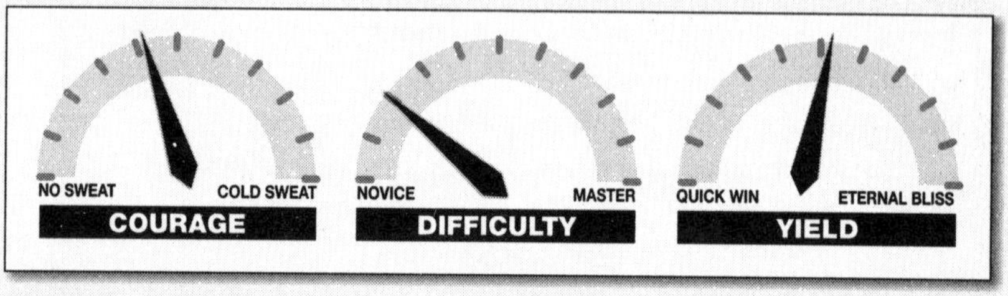

STEPS: 5

TAKEAWAY: You have to change how you scan

KEEPING SCORE: Are you a victim, just coping, or are you a Pushback Zealot?

WHY DO LESS

Email and the myriad other ways of connecting with anyone anywhere, are both a blessing and a curse.

• The upside: They bring the world to you.

• The downside: They bring the noisy, unfiltered, unfocused, and undesired world to you! •

You need to get disciplined about closing your virtual door

HOW TO DO LESS

1

Let's say it together...

Hi.

My name is ______, and I have a Scanning Problem.

My first step on the road to recovery is admitting it.

Great! You're on your way!

Yes, *they* shouldn't send so much, and they should be clearer, and do a better job of labeling and organizing whatever they send out. But *they* won't. So, since the clutter and crap you receive is only going to get worse, it's time to deal with it.

Yes, technology is part of the solution. You need better spam filters. (See Bonus Step below.)

But like most twelve-step change programs (which I've simplified to five), the first step in eliminating most of the noise coming at you is admitting that you own part of the problem. If you are like most people, you were never taught to quickly scan and edit massive amounts of information *before* getting sucked into the minutia of each message. The key to continuously eliminating three-quarters of what comes at you is accepting that you have to change how you scan information.

And not just the stuff from "outsiders." It is supercritical that you also change how you scan messages from your company, teammates, and buddies too.

2

Scanning Simplified...

Getting good at scanning everything that comes at you can (and should) take years. This is a stopgap solution until you build that skill.

If BOTH the Subject and the Sender fail to create this reaction:

I have to read or at least scan this today....

DO NOT open or scan the message. Hit Delete immediately.

We all read messages because we know the sender — email has been called the killer app because it so easily connects us to others. And we all dig into emails that help us manage our daily to-do's — most of us use email as a task management tool. And we continuously bounce back and forth: opening one email because it's from a buddy, and the next because it relates to our work. Unfortunately, most of our bouncing is unfocused and undisciplined. Get proactive by making BOTH the Subject and Sender ring your chimes before you consider reading on. If only the Subject OR the Sender do it for you, hit Delete.

•

This strategy will empty at least 50% of your in-box before you begin truly paying attention.[1]

(If following this strategy makes you nervous, re-read Chapter 1. You'll learn why savvy employees are ruthless about how much goes into their Trash box.)

❸

Scan the remaining messages for two bits of information:

- Action you must take
- Date or deadline for that action, within the next two to three weeks

If the messages do not contain an action and a short-term date, delete them. (See…Chapter 1 follows you!)

•

At this point, your in-box should be at least 75% emptied.[2]

•

Time commitment for Steps 2 and 3 combined:

Maximum: 10 minutes

Now you're ready to begin paying full attention to whatever's coming at you. But if you'd like to pay attention to *even less*…

4

Scan the remaining messages using the CLEAR model.
The information within the message must provide or be:

- **C**onnected — to your current projects and workload
- **L**ist next steps — What you should do after reading the email
- **E**xpectations — What success looks like
- **A**bility — How you'll get things done: lists tools and support
- **R**eturn — Your WIIFM: answers "What's in it for me?"

If the message does not meet CLEAR criteria, hit Delete or tell the sender you need these five points before you can respond properly.

•

After CLEAR, your in-box should be at least 90% emptied.[3]

•

So, why isn't the title of this chapter *How to Delete 90% of Your Emails*? Because I've learned something about human nature.

The CLEAR model appeared in my first book, *Simplicity*. Since then, people have raved about its effectiveness: "So simple, yet so rigorous!" Yet when I followed up with them, only a small percentage had kept using it beyond a few months. Consistent use of the CLEAR model means making a commitment to be disciplined about scanning information. And the simple truth is that few of us really want to be that disciplined. If you're ready to make that commitment, a lot less awaits you — 90% less.

Even without Step 4: A 75% emptied in-box ain't bad! Shoot for that!

(For more about the power and effectiveness of the CLEAR model, see Chapter 5)

5

If the advice in this chapter makes you squirm with "Yeah, but's"... and "This won't work because...": Use common sense.

Of course there are times where this approach might trash an important email. Of course, on occasion, you should make exceptions. My advice from years of watching people dealing with overload: DO NOT make exceptions right away. If you do, you'll quickly return to being a slave to all your exceptions. Instead, try this:

- Adhere to Steps 1–3 for a month, placing all deleted emails in a Hold box instead of Trash
- Then, at the end of the trial, examine how many of those emails truly deserved your attention

I guarantee you'll be surprised at how few exceptions were really necessary! And you can then use what you've discovered as part of your revised scanning strategy.

❻ Bonus Step

Get a spam filter...Now!

If you work in a small firm, there's no excuse for not implementing this step immediately. Simply ask a techie friend for advice, or do a search for *spam filter* on Google.

Jupiter Research estimates that by 2006, consumers can expect 1,400 pieces of junk email per year.[4] From our experience with knowledge- and service-workers, that number is way-low! During July, 2002, anti-spam service provider Brightmail, which at the time was scanning more than 2 billion emails every month, estimated that unsolicited bulk email made up a whopping 36 percent of all email traveling over the Internet.[5] And in July, 2003, Nucleus Research estimated that companies lose 1.4% of each employee's productivity each year due to spam — costing $874 per employee per year.[6] This problem is bad, and it's only gonna get worse. Protect yourself now.

If you work in a larger firm, this may be tougher — you'll have to work within your techno-wonk's priority and vendor lists. Don't give up. Beg, cry, suck up, or even offer questionable forms of bribery if you must. Getting a spam filter is that important!

The Power of Scanning Strategies[7]

EMAILS DELETED or IGNORED *before* paying any attention	SCANNING STRATEGY	TRAITS	PERCENTAGE OF POPULATION
< 50%	**Victim**	Attempts to be pragmatic; Evaluates too many incoming messages; Has no concise scanning or reading strategy	**40%**
50%	**Just Coping**	Spends too much time on the ***wrong*** emails. (Many teammate/boss/company messages can be ignored.) Keeps up with daily onslaught, but rarely "clears the plate."	**50%**
75%	**Proactive**	Has a concise scanning and reading strategy. Is surgical when deleting more than 50% of emails; Makes time to pay attention to remaining 25%	**8%**
90%	**Pushback Zealot**	Very disciplined and consistent; Uses freed time to focus on new projects, new opportunities, new people	**2%**

WHAT'S BEHIND DOING LESS

You probably read this chapter searching for a solution to in-box overload.

Yet, if you're like most people we've interviewed, that's not your real problem. You are likely a victim of what Gartner Research calls "pervasive connectivity" — the ability of anyone to reach you at any time. And while I've focused this chapter solely on emails, the challenges and solutions also apply to cell phones, instant messaging, and a slew of other ways that people reach you. **Pervasive connectivity** preys upon our weaknesses:

- Instant-access technology has created an implied need to be available to everyone, respond to everything, and do so quickly.

Those who can't get past that absurdly unrealistic expectation suffer from constant burnout.

- Few of us were ever taught how to quickly scan and edit massive amounts of information using objective criteria. Most of us use a patchwork of coping techniques, laden with personal biases that do as much harm as good.

•

A generational thing? There is mounting evidence that Baby Boomers are most afflicted with this problem and that members of Gen Y, those born after 1980 — (because they were the first generation where the Internet was "always there") — seem better equipped to manage connectivity overload. However, don't cheer for Gen Y just yet. In the past decade I have interviewed hundreds of teachers. Many of them have expressed a concern that this generation is not learning the deep critical-thinking skills they will need — scanning, synthesizing, analyzing, organizing, clarifying, etc. — to keep pace with pervasive connectivity. The next decade will demonstrate whether or not that's a valid concern.

•

Most connectivity demons are personal. Don't look to business to solve them

In 1997, I was invited to present the research we had done on work complexity to the Conference Board's Council on Development, Education, and Training. These were 30 of the top people in their field: I thought, surely, they would know what to do with the demons of pervasive connectivity and overload. After five hours of presenting data and brainstorming new solutions, the most promising comment I heard was "Gee, maybe we should spend a little less on executive education, and a little more on all employees."

But the naivete was mine, not theirs. Expecting business to deal with employees' gaps in scanning and listening strategies is like expecting them to boil the ocean. It just isn't going to happen. Most of the demons associated with the noise coming at you are your own, that you must deal with, not your company's.

•

Killer InfoGlut is coming!
Prepare now

This is only gonna get worse! IM (instant messaging) offers you less time and information to make your decisions — an estimated 84% of North American companies already use it[8] — and SMS (short messaging service, a mobile technology) is quickly becoming the connection-of-choice outside of the U.S. Other new technologies and information applications are on the horizon, ensuring that you will soon refer to your current overload problems as the Good Old Days.

Remember that the steps in this chapter are just stopgap solutions. If you are going to remain employable, you'll need to build a portfolio of enhanced skills, and high on the list is improving how you scan information.

“ ” QUOTE OF NOTE

Pervasive connectivity implies pervasive accessibility... It lays the onus on people to disconnect before they burn out.
GARTNER RESEARCH

WANT MORE?

Use this chapter as a jumping off point for building your own personal scanning and listening strategy. Only you can determine what works for you, which virtual doors can be closed and how to close them. (For example, no one — not even family — has my cell phone number. I use it only for outgoing calls, and manage incoming messages through office voicemail. That's one part of my personalized strategy. What's yours?) For more tips about dealing with email and connectivity overload — like using multiple email addresses for different purposes, staying out of back-and-forth conversations that generate endless streams of emails, using Web sites for sharing attachments, and more:

- www.email911.com
- www.overcomeemailoverload.com
- *Turn It Off: How to Unplug from the Anytime-Anywhere Office Without Disconnecting Your Career* by Gil Gordon

3

How to
Quickly Prepare to Communicate with Anyone, About Anything

Note: You're *not yet communicating...* This is just how to *prepare.*

LESS•O•METERS

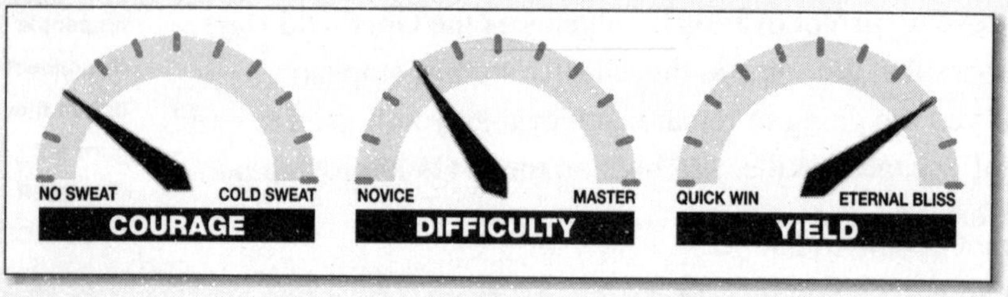

STEPS: 3

TAKEAWAY: Know, Feel, Do is speed-freak clarity

KEEPING SCORE: This is guaranteed to work — if you're disciplined. Will you be?

WHY DO LESS

Your normal day: Tyranny of the Urgent • You've got only seconds — on a good day, maybe minutes — to organize your thoughts, shape your message, and get clear • You need the absolute shortest path between what's in your head and what others will see or hear

HOW TO DO LESS

Pre-Work

Always remember three words:

- **Know**
- **Feel**
- **Do**

With very little practice, Know, Feel, Do will help create instant clarity in any situation.

1

KNOW:

"What's the one thing I want people to know, understand, learn, or question?"

Your answer should be no longer than one sentence.
Write it down.

2

FEEL:

"How do I want people to feel when I'm done?"

Your answer should be no longer than one sentence.
Write it down.
While you can't mandate how people will feel — ("Be happy, dammit!") — this reminds you to prepare for the emotional impact of your words, possibly changing your delivery.

3

DO:

"What do I want people to do as a direct result of my communication?"

Your answer should be no longer than one sentence.
Write it down.

•

Time to go through these three steps

Initially: 1–10 minutes
With practice: 45 seconds or less

Why Know, Feel, Do Works

First, it's short, easy to remember, and easy to complete, even under pressure. I have known harried managers who have scribbled three sentences while dashing between meetings, and during meetings — just moments before they were supposed to speak — and as rough-text in an email. Think of Know, Feel, Do as speed-freak clarity.

Second, it's disciplined and addictive. People who practice Know, Feel, Do find it easier to remain disciplined about how they communicate, and confess that the times they have lacked clarity were the times they hadn't done this homework.

Most important: It "forces" you to see your audience as decision-makers, and to organize your thoughts *according to how they listen.* In a hurried, get-it-done-now workplace, most everyone wants every communicator to

- "Get to the point!
  What's the one thing you want me to remember?" (Know)
- "Show me you care about my needs." (Feel)
- "Be clear about what I'm supposed to do next." (Do)

Know, Feel, Do is a concise preparation tool for communicating in any morebetterfaster environment. (For more, see Chapters 4 and 5.)

Why It's So Important

Every day, you must communicate to tens or hundreds or thousands of people who are instantly deciding whether they buy into whatever you're saying, and whether they should act. Most will give you only seconds to grab their attention and convince them. Lack of clarity and focus has been called the Silent Career Killer. Few in your audience will tell you that you were unclear. But they'll remember! We must all compete on clarity. Every day.

EXAMPLE: LESS PREP, MO' IMPACT

(OK, I'm cheating with more than one sentence. Cut me some slack, please. An example in a book needs to be more detailed than a note written to yourself.)

Know the plan

- Understand the specifics of our new plan and their role in its success
- Understand how we are defining success for this particular change effort

Feel excited as well as accountable

- Excited about clearer goals and knowing next steps
- Accountable for removing barriers for successful implementation

Do what it takes

- Attend a training session
- Use the information I've provided to accomplish (such-and-such) tasks

WHAT'S BEHIND DOING LESS

Know, Feel, Do was born at a **communication crash site**. During our research, we found that people-oriented processes kept slamming into get-it-done-now juggernauts.

Early in the 1990s, change management practitioners applied a very powerful change model — Head, Heart, and Hands. The idea elegantly described how to create sustainable change:

- People need to understand the rationale behind change, and they need to come to their own conclusions. Thus *head*.
- And they need to actively participate in the process of making decisions, creating their own buy-in…*heart*.
- Finally, they need the right tools to implement the change… *hands*.

Great model! However, its application became a problem. Change gurus took everyone offsite for days at a time with lots of hand-holding, singing of songs, and group-gropes dressed as team-building exercises. The get-it-done-now forces (usually at the top of the organization) pushed back, demanding ever-shorter communication and engagement cycles.

In studying that collision, we found that a lot of the processing time (but not all) could be eliminated if those driving the change condensed and focused their communication. We asked some executives and change agents to reduce their entire process down to just three sentences. At that moment the Head, Heart, Hand model became Know, Feel, Do.

Know, Feel, Do works because it's the shortest distance between what's in your head and what people need to see or hear — that still respects the very personal needs of your audience. Rarely do journalistic models (Who/What/Where, etc.) or strategic planning models (Mission/Focus/Priorities) or operational models (Goals/Measures, etc.) prepare you to connect with the *person* on the other side of your communication.

•

Important Tip: Don't talk at people. Have a conversation.
Ideally, your three sentences will help you frame a dialogue, not a download.

WANT MORE?

Additional examples of Know, Feel, Do can be found at www.simplerwork.com

How to **Leave Shorter Voicemails for Better Results**

LESS•O•METERS

STEPS: 3

TAKEAWAY: Know, Feel, Do to the rescue

KEEPING SCORE: Win in 30, or face electronic death

WHY DO LESS

99.999%* of all voicemails should not exceed 30 seconds in length • Under 20 seconds is preferable • The key is in knowing how to use that time • Those who do know how get their messages heard, returned, and acted upon

* No, I can't validate this percentage. But you got the point, right?

HOW TO DO LESS

1

Always assume:

Nobody answers their phone anymore –
you will automatically go into voicemail

If you begin with that assumption, three things have already happened:

- You will be thinking about your message *before* the b-e-e-p
- You are ahead of more than half of all message-leavers[1], who scramble at the b-e-e-p, searching for the right words
- If someone *does* pick up, you'll sound amazingly focused and articulate

2

Always remember three words:

- **Know**
- **Feel**
- **Do**

Pop Quiz: Do you know why? See page 28

2 a

"Hello, Joe. Here's the one thing I want you to know." (Know)

Maybe not phrased that way…But because nobody has time to listen for more than one — possibly two — points in a voicemail, know that point before you dial.

2 b

Your tone of voice can impact when your call gets returned. (Feel)

Depending on circumstances, three tones-of-voice create the fastest replies[2]:

- High energy [+]
  Messages that ooooze endorphins and adrenaline
- Happiness [+]
  Tip from acting coaches: Smile when leaving a message. The tone of your voice will change!

- Frustration or feigned helplessness [–]
  If you want immediate corrective action or you're going for the sympathy vote ("Helllllllp!"), a tone of concern works wonders. (If frustrated, be firm but polite. Never angry.)

2 C

"Joe, here's what I need you to do." (Do)

Short. Clear. Two to three sentences, maximum.

3

Leave your phone number.

Always say it at the speed of handwriting, not talking

Unless you speak with this person every day, never assume they have your phone number at their fingertips. And say it slowly enough for someone to write it down without replaying your message several times.

•

Time commitment for Steps 1 through 3:
Maximum: 30 seconds

•

If more than 30 seconds are required (for greater detail), send them an email, or package, or deliver the message in-person instead. Or leave a voicemail asking to schedule that face-to-face meeting.

[" "]

VOX POP

Well, duhhhh!

TELEMARKETING MANAGER

who believes these tips should be self-evident to anyone who's ever used a phone

WHAT'S BEHIND DOING LESS

I confess that, in the past, my reaction has been similar to the telemarketer above: **"This is a no-brainer. Must we talk about this?"**

But I've learned that we must. Far too many people think out loud, ramble, and blabber while leaving messages. ("Well, we had this team meeting. And Harvey — you remember Harvey? He said that you knew somebody who knew somebody…") Or, um, worse, um, can't seem to remember why they are calling, or, um, are clearly unprepared to use anyone's time and attention.

•

Universal Rules of the Game[3]

- **There is a 15-Second Penalty Box**
  Your first 5 to 15 seconds are critical. That's when most listeners decide to Delete, Forward, Save (for "Whenever"), or Respond
- **Win in 30, Or Face Electronic Death**
  If you haven't nailed your point within 30 seconds, most listeners have either deleted your message, or are wishing they could
- **Winning Isn't Just Beating the Clock**
  Great voicemails provide the right information in the right way. Clearly. Wonderfully. Effectively. (Which translates to: Know, Feel, Do)
- **You Are Being Squeezed-In**
  Most people check their voicemails during time-bound moments. Like in between back-to-back meetings, when running through an airport or boarding a plane, in between bites of a sandwich, etc.

Understand and work within these rules, and you'll be a cherished teammate. Ignore them at your own peril.

5

How to
Write Shorter Emails for Better Results

LESS•O•METERS

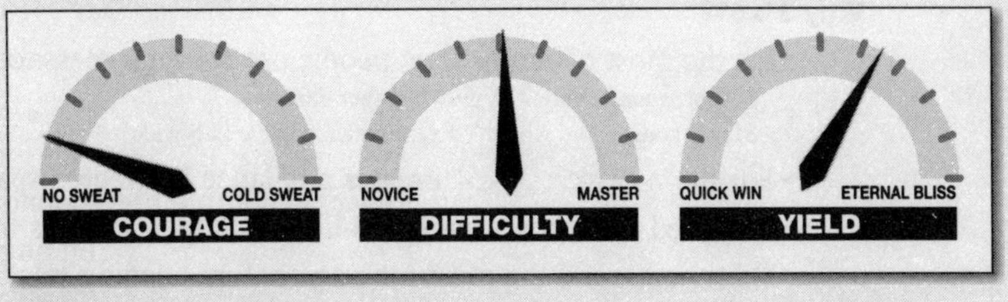

STEPS: 4

TAKEAWAY: CLEAR produces awesome results

KEEPING SCORE: Did you grab their attention and make it easy to understand and act?

WHY DO LESS

Voicemails are restricted by time • Emails by space • You must grab someone's attention, connect with them, and help them commit to action — all within 3"X5" • Otherwise, you will be among their 75% deleted messages

HOW TO DO LESS

1

Anything worth reading MUST fit in the top 3"x5"

Newspaper journalists are taught to write by visualizing an inverted pyramid: Most critical facts and emotional connections are always at the top of the story. "Filler" details run at the bottom. That way, if the story must be cut, entire paragraphs can be lopped off, always from the bottom.

Same thing applies to emails. Most critical facts and emotional connections go up top. Detailed information and explanations down below.

Why 3"x5"?

- It's the most common size* people use for their message window[1]

  * Approximate. Varies slightly in either direction.
  Metric conversion: About 7.5 centimeters high x 12.5 wide
- For the receiver: 3"x5" creates a balance between a space designed for fast scanning (as little as 2 to 3 seconds for skilled skimmers), and the most message before needing to scroll.[2]
- Think of being disciplined about 3"x5" as training for the extreme space constraints of instant messages, Blackberries, and cell phones.

2

You are writing a billboard. Not a letter.

Write for easy scanning

While every message is unique, scan-friendly tips include:

- No more than 75 to 110 words in the top 3"x5" (About 8 to 12 sentences, the fewer the better)
- Break anything longer than 3 lines with bullets and/or white space
- Set for auto-wrap or hit Return after 8 to 10 words (for shorter line lengths and easier readability)

See example.

3

Always use the CLEAR model.

Receivers are scanning your messages for these points:

- **C**onnected — to their current projects and workload
- **L**ist next steps — What you want them to do after reading your email
- **E**xpectations — What success looks like
- **A**bility — How they'll get things done: lists tools and support
- **R**eturn — Their WIIFM: answers "What's in it for me?"

•

Why is it critical to be CLEAR?

Know, Feel, Do seems like a simpler framework: it's shorter and it works for voicemails! Why not use it? Different rules for different media.

People scan visual information differently. Even with minimal word-counts, they expect extremely useful details — *especially if you are asking them to do something*. Then, your job is to help them make an informed decision. Remember Darwinian Law! It's not just the shortest emails that survive, but the fittest.

4

Use common sense

Of course there are times when two-word replies, or rambling prose, or other exceptions apply. The advice in this chapter isn't about one formula for all emails. It's about discipline. Get *disciplined* in delivering the most robust and valued information within the smallest possible space, and you'll be a cherished teammate. Every time.

Anatomy of a CLEAR Email

Your mini-billboard can grab attention as well as influence behaviors.
The secrets are in the nuances and details of being CLEAR.

Subject

[1] `Project XYZ: Next Steps` **[2]**

Text

```
Anne:

Hi!
Great meeting last week! Thanks for the 40-hr days you
must be putting in. I hope Harry understands all you're
doing for him! [3]

Attached: Rough draft [4] of what we owe him. Could you
take a look at it? [5]

After you're dazzled by my brilliance in this draft...[6]
  • Please critique pages 7-8, 23-24 [7]

I think those are the places Harry will check to see if
we're meeting his needs. [8]

Give me a call by next Tuesday [9] and we'll talk through
to-do's. We can get this off your plate within two
weeks! [10]

Enjoy! Bill J
```

[1] "Project XYZ" says to Anne: This is **Connected to what you do** — your current project.

[2] "Next Steps" says: Read Me. I'm about to **List next steps** — stuff you've got to do. If you refer back to Chapter 2, you'll recall why Subject lines like this one are so critical.

[3 & 6] In Chapters 3 and 4, we reviewed the importance of **emotional tone**. These four sentences make a personal connection with Anne. Stroking works! Do it.

[4] Anne's **Ability** to respond on time (by next Tuesday) is directly connected to the attached rough draft. The draft document is a tool to jumpstart her efforts. Other tools and support could have included:

- Scheduling a meeting before Tuesday to brainstorm solutions

- Providing contact information of others who could help her
- Directing her to existing research materials, etc.

...anything that would help her or expedite her to-do's

5] "Could you take a look at it?" is one of Anne's **Listed next steps**

7] "Please critique" is one of Anne's **Listed next steps**

8] True to real-life in many companies, you'll notice that **Expectations** — successful completion of this project — do not involve corporate measures. In this email, meeting expectations means keeping Harry happy!

9] "Give me a call" is Anne's final **Listed next steps**

0] What's the **Return** to Anne for taking on this assignment? What's *her* WIIFM? Not fame, glory, or a raise. Merely "getting this off your plate within two weeks." For harried and Harry'd Anne, making something go away within two weeks is a very good thing.

CLEAR Stats

- This email has 98 words
- Only 10 sentences
- **Yet it delivered** all five points people scan for, and struck an emotional chord — all within 3"x5". With practice, you can accomplish even more in less space.

WHAT'S BEHIND DOING LESS

Influencing Other People's Behaviors

Since 1992, as part of *The Search for a Simpler Way*, we have seen one factor increasingly dominate and drive human behavior within companies — how people's time and attention are used and respected.

Thousands of interview responses sound like this one from an automobile executive: "To be honest, the work I do first is not what's on the strategic plan or tracked by our measures. I do whatever's easiest to 'check off' first. And whatever's easiest has usually been presented to me in ways that are easy to understand and pay attention to. I don't have time to figure out most of what comes at me. Whoever makes it easiest to respond, gets my attention."

[" "]

QUOTE OF NOTE

If it's short, it's more likely to actually be used. If something requires a large investment of time — or looks like it will —it's less likely to be used.

STEVE KRUG

Don't Make Me Think

And like this, from a pet-food manager: "I just keep doing things the way I've been doing them because I don't have the time to figure out all these convoluted changes they keep sending at me."

Hearing responses like these again and again drove me to jot down the first of three Laws of Workplace Behavior: Make it easier for people to do things your way, and you'll get your way more often. Ease-of-use and reduced-use-of-time are *huge* drivers of human behavior! (See Laws•O•Less box, page 43.)

Obvious, right? Yet the main reason this book exists is that most of us violate this law most of the time! If you reflect on the best and worst practices you have witnessed — in making presentations, running meetings, clarifying goals, and more — you'll find that *every best practice* is grounded in saving people time or making things easier to use. And that every *worst* practice ignores these guiding principles.

Bringing it back to shorter, more effective emails, as well as any communication:

Treating people's time and attention as precious
is directly connected to the effectiveness of your communication

Please consider that fact every time you hit Send.

•

CLEAR:

The shortest path to committed action

CLEAR is not just a cute mnemonic device to help you to remember to be clear. It is heavily researched and anchored in human behavior.

By 1994, as part of our study, we noticed a pattern in most everyone's decision-making process. When people have an exchange with someone else (*any* exchange — emails, one-on-one conversations, group meetings, phone calls), and they are…

- Asked to take action, participate, cooperate, or make a commitment

Their decision to

- Do nothing or resist…
- Act, but only by complying…or
- Act with full commitment…

is based upon five separate criteria which buzz through their brains in nanoseconds. We labeled these criteria Behavioral Communication. If you want someone to make a committed decision to act, you need to answer five key questions:

BEHAVIORAL COMMUNICATION **The anatomy of any committed decision to act**	**CLEAR** **Influencing how others make decisions** Your communication must convey
• How is this relevant to what I do?	**C**onnection to their workload
• What, specifically, should I do?	**L**ist action steps
• What do success and failure look like?	**E**xpectations for success
• What tools and support are available?	**A**bility to achieve success
• WIIFM — What's in it for me?	**R**eturn to that person

Between 1994 and 2003, my teammates and I tested the five questions of Behavioral Communication with over 300,000 people in 17 countries. (From formal surveys and interviews to show-of-hands responses in workshops.) Language and cultural differences have created variations in how each question is phrased, but the validity of the model has not wavered:

> When people choose between doing nothing, acting by complying, or committing to act, **they consistently make their decisions based on the answers they get to the five questions of Behavioral Communication.**

So, if you're seeking committed behaviors — whether through emails, face-to-face conversations, presentations, or any other form of communication — you better figure out how you're gonna answer those questions! And, after years of testing, I can promise you that CLEAR is the shortest path you'll take. **CLEAR makes it easy for others to commit to act, not just comply.**

One last promise: Want to skip over some of the five points so you can communicate faster? Go ahead! But here's a guarantee… Instead of just one round of emails, respondents will come back to you twice, thrice, up to five times — until their behavioral questions are answered. One email or five, it's your choice.

WANT MORE?

Additional Email Basic Tips

- See Chapter 2
- Go to www.simplerwork.com for additional basic tips

Tear-Out Tools

See Do-Less Toolkit on page 265 for tear-out versions of

- CLEAR
- Behavioral Communication
- All three Laws of Workplace Behavior

For Quick Lesson in How Emails Go Public

- Go to www.internalmemos.com

  Your latest email may already be posted!

  If not, you can enjoy other people's follies. Like CEO Julie engaging in back-and-forth rants with her employees: "I see that whoever has been sending our emails to a certain website, has done it again. I am not amused by this." Quite funny! Unless, of course, you are Julie.

For those who noticed: Behavioral Communication was first widely publicized in *Simplicity* in 2000. The third question was listed as "How will I be measured, and what are the consequences?" — which limited its use to workplaces. The broader use of the model by *Simplicity* readers changed the wording to be more applicable in any situation. Same universal question, just phrased differently.

Laws•O•Less

There are three places in this book where the tips for doing less soar beyond the boundaries of that chapter. They offer guiding principles, foundations — laws — that influence our everyday lives. This is the first of those places. **There's a lot more here than just shorter emails!**

Ease-of-use and reduced-use-of-time are equal to — and sometimes more important than — recognition, compassion, inclusion, rewards, penalties, loyalty, and hierarchy in their ability to drive human behaviors.

The So What? Law of Doing Less

Make it easier for people to do things your way, and you'll get your way more often.

The Search for a Simpler Way: Almost immediately, we began to see how many behaviors were driven by how easy or hard it was to "check off" to-do's. So between 1998–2003, during interviews with more than 1,000 people, we asked such questions as "Which tasks do you do first, or last, or postpone for as long as you can? Why?" Combined with other data, such as usability studies of worktools and process designs, what evolved was the first of three Laws of Workplace Behavior, above.

6

How to
Do Less and Still Deliver an Awesome Presentation

LESS•O•METERS

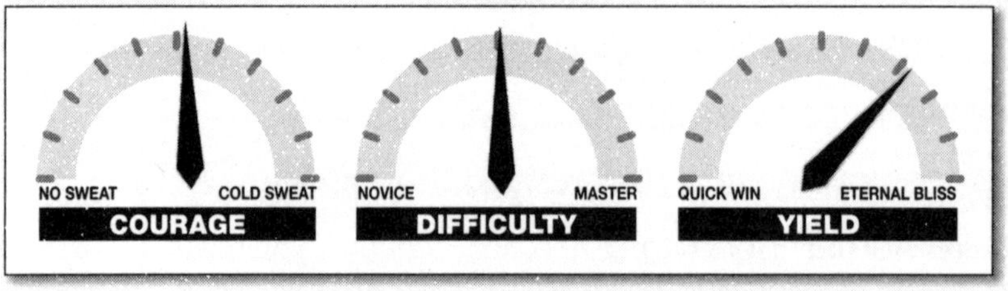

STEPS: 3

TAKEAWAY: Never "present"— always provoke conversations

KEEPING SCORE: Great presentations change the conversation afterwards

WHY DO LESS

PowerPoint* is

a) Among mankind's worst inventions, ever • It is the largest single source of useless crap within companies

b) A wonderful presentation tool that's only as good as you are

c) Both A and B

* While this tool is particularly odious, feel free to substitute any presentation media. A–C above still apply.

HOW TO DO LESS

Pre-Work

Last Time...Always remember three words:

- **Know** • **Feel** • **Do**

I say *last time** only because you are surely expecting more than one how-to, repeated over and over. So: The very first step — *before* booting up PowerPoint or picking up a marker — is to get clear on

- The one thing you want people to remember from your presentation
- How the experience will feel for them, and
- The one thing you want them to do as a direct result of your presentation

If I thought you would tolerate even greater repetition of this pre-work, I'd do it!

Twenty-four of thirty-three chapters are about how you relate to others, connect with them, and share ideas with them. In every instance — emails, presentations, job interviews, performance reviews, and more — the first step towards doing less and accomplishing more is for you to get clear about what you want people to *Know, Feel*, and *Do*. That clarity will always serve you well.

(**Last time* refers only to reminding you of required pre-work…you will still see these three words again!)

1

Turn the one point you want people to KNOW into a QUESTION. Turn the question into an interactive exercise with the audience

There are two reasons for this approach:

You do less work. In a one-hour presentation, the norm is for you to spend 50 minutes presenting, and 10 minutes on audience Q&A. Most people think that means they've got to prepare 50 minutes worth of material. Wrong!

If you turn the top one or two major points of your presentation into questions, and involve the audience — by talking among themselves and then "reporting out" their responses — the time you spend talking will be closer to 30 or 40 minutes.

The audience helps you build your presentation, and it's a lot easier to get people talking to each other than it is to be brilliant, witty, and responsive during that 10 minute Q&A session.

You get better audience reaction. Unless you are a truly gifted speaker, people do not want to be *presented to*. They want your key points, a few details, and the opportunity to internalize them, and dig deeper. If you turn those key points into questions, you create a win-win: Less work for you, and more audience satisfaction.

(For more, see example.)

2

Did you catch the radical idea in Step 1?

Never "present."

Always provoke conversations

While you cannot ignore the standard measures of your success — smile-sheet scores, or delivering new information, or reinforcing whatever your boss wants you to say — they have little to do with the true effectiveness of your presentation.

Your true success is measured by changes in conversation. Good presentations create dialogue in the room, in the moment. Great presentations change the conversation afterwards.

That's when people change their decisions, priorities, and actions. So the real measure of your effectiveness is in how people's conversations were changed by what you said and did. If your definition of success includes "What will people talk about after my presentation, that they weren't talking about before?" you will find yourself doing less "presenting" and more interactive provoking of conversations.

3

If you must use PowerPoint...

(Movie clips, computer animation, and images instead of words are often better in today's Attention Deficit Society. And nothing at all — just you with a few reminder notes — is also great. Still, the ubiquity and ease-of-use of PowerPoint makes it likely that you'll be doing many a text- and numbers-based slide show.)

please demonstrate respect and care for your audience. Always...

3 a

Create a one-page summary

No matter how brief your presentation, no matter how focused, everybody always wants the Cut-to-the-Chase, Spell-Everything-Out-in-One-Page Summary. (This is *not* an outline of your key points. Create a *What This Means to You* one-pager for your audience. For more how-to specifics, see Chapter 9.)

3 b

Use a 1:3 ratio to determine slide count

If your slides include mostly text, numbers, and tables/charts, you should present a *maximum* of one slide every three minutes. (One hour presentation = 20 slides maximum, half-hour = 10, etc.) Why? A 1:3 ratio imposes self-discipline. Communication discipline. You are "forced" to take the time to explain, illuminate, and connect the ideas on each slide. (See Chapter 9 for more. Including advice to use even *fewer* slides.)

3 c

Insist that everyone get handouts.

Ideally, before you present, not afterwards

Learning Theory 101: The more you can integrate what and how people see, hear, and take notes, the better your message will be understood, retained, discussed, and acted upon.

Example: Present Less, Ask More

(For all audiences except senior execs. For presenting to them, see Chapter 9)

From

Our Strategy

- These are gazillions of
- bullet points about our strategy
- and not once
- will I ever stop to ask you,
- the audience,
- what you think

TALKING AT PEOPLE

- Most presenters believe more is better: "I know I can convince you of my point if I squeeze 4,327 slides into this 15-minute presentation."

To

Our Strategy

Now that I've laid out the five key ideas in our strategy:

- How does that change the work done by your team?
- How does it change how we coordinate all of our efforts?

ENGAGING PEOPLE IN CONVERSATION

- Spend less time making key points
- More time engaging people in what those points mean to them
- This is how presentation effectiveness often skyrockets
- Have audience members talk among themselves for 5 to 10 minutes, in groups of 6 to 12 people—addressing the question(s) you posed to them. Then ask a sample of those in the room to "report out" what they discussed. You just reduced a lot of your presentation time!
- Note: The questions do not have to be answered in full *during* your presentation. Your goal is to help change what people talk about *after* your presentation

WHAT'S BEHIND DOING LESS

IBM lore includes a story of a technological failure that helped launch cultural change. A projector broke just as a manager was making his first presentation to newly-appointed CEO Lou Gerstner. The befuddled manager didn't know what to do without his *foils*. **"Just talk to me,"** said Gerstner. From that point forward, no manager could hide behind a presentation.

A fitting story to remember. Because, unfortunately, the business of business seems to be making presentations to each other. The art of creating clarity and connecting with people is being replaced with the art of making slides. PowerPoint and similar tools are clogging our companies with more clutter and crap than illumination.

I do not make these disparaging generalizations lightly. Two trends are universal:

- The number of presentations managers and executives make keeps increasing every year — some report as much as a ten-fold increase in as many years.
- Preparation time has changed dramatically: There's greater emphasis on the creation of slides and other media, with less and less time allowed for speaker preparation.

I witnessed one internal presentation — a senior executive talking to 500 managers — with 137 slides shown in 52 minutes. The record in our interviews: 108 slides in 25 minutes. (That's one slide every 13.9 seconds — mostly text and tables!) And this isn't just a top-down problem. I recently worked with a middle-management team in a Fortune 250 company that needed to make a critical presentation to their senior team. We spent a full day paring their presentation down to 12 slides, with lots of time available for discussion with the executives. Nonetheless, the final presentation ballooned back to 41 slides with almost no discussion.

C'mon!

Do less *presenting* and more *engaging*. For your own sake, focus less on quantity of slides and more on quality of conversation.

•

Good presentations create dialogue in the room, in the moment. Great presentations change the conversation afterwards.
A major healthcare and consumer products firm recently hired an executive to reinvent their approach to product innovation. At first, his presentations talked about — what else? — innovation. But he found that most of his teammates didn't have a good grounding in their customers' needs. So he stopped talking about innovation, and started sharing customer feedback. (He did Step 1: Turning what *customers* wanted the company to KNOW into questions, such as "Why would they say this product doesn't meet their needs? It's our best-seller!")

His questions sparked debates that spilled into the halls and into other meetings. *He changed what people talked about*. That changed how they approached innovation. And that changed their success rate in new product launches by 150%! **Your true success is measured by changes in conversation.**

Every day, employees are overloaded with mind-numbing data-dumps, when what they really need are clarifying conversations, and opportunities to make sense of the material that is presented to them.

No question that making your presentation more responsive to those needs may take some skill-building. It's a lot easier to compose and click through slides than it is to figure out how to engage people in what you have to say. (To build those skills, see *Want More?*)

Yet the tougher challenge in doing less is having the courage of your own convictions. Saying less means greater accountability for whatever you do say. Saying less means actually thinking instead of just creating slides. And, like taking a stand in any environment, it exposes you to question and debate — but question and debate that will be far more productive for you and your audience than any PowerPoint presentation can claim.

Your future foretold

Fourth-graders in Bolivar Intermediate School in Missouri make their presentations in PowerPoint. "They're visually stimulated — that's the way their brains are wired," says their teacher, Shane Medlin. Even second graders are using it. Exciting future, yes?

Maybe. Another grade-school teacher, Daniel Zittoun of Madison, Connecticut, says that the graphics are so eye-catching "you can forget to look at the content."[1] Concern about the use of PowerPoint in schools is growing. Says Peter McGrath, past president of the University of Missouri and the University of Minnesota, "Writing has eroded seriously."[2] A hint of presentations to come….

WANT MORE?

Basic Tips

- www.simplerwork.com for more tips and sample presentations
- Gettysburg Address in PowerPoint: http://www.norvig.com/Gettysburg/index.htm
  Biting satire! How the ultimate standard in brilliance, simplicity, and clarity can be beaten to death by slides
- *Really Bad PowerPoint (and How to Avoid It),* by Seth Godin, Amazon e-doc
- *On Writing Well,* by William K. Zinsser
  Presenting and writing both require getting clear. This is one of the bibles on clarity!

Power Tips

Once you move beyond slide shows, you're open to a new world of possibilities! Among them…

Storytelling

Some basic truths: When making sense of things, we listen for narratives. Listening to an argument or rationale makes us a critic, while a story makes us a participant. Stories make the abstract concrete, they engage people at all levels of their being —mind, emotions, and actions. (There's Know, Feel, Do again!) People use stories to make sense of the present, past, and future, to make disparate elements whole. A starter kit:

- *Simplicity,* by Bill Jensen, plus www.simplerwork.com
- *The Springboard,* by Stephen Denning

Conversations and Questions

People tolerate management's logic, but they act on their own conclusions. A slide-after-slide presentation is *your* logic. Your audience needs conversation in order to come to their own conclusions. A starter kit:

- *Turning to One Another,* by Margaret J. Wheatley
- *Encyclopedia of Positive Questions, Volume I,* by Diana L. Whitney, et al.

Large Group Facilitation

A starter kit:

- *Open Space Technology,* by Harrison Owen
- www.openspaceworld.org

7

How to
Go to Fewer Meetings and Get More Out of Them

LESS•O•METERS

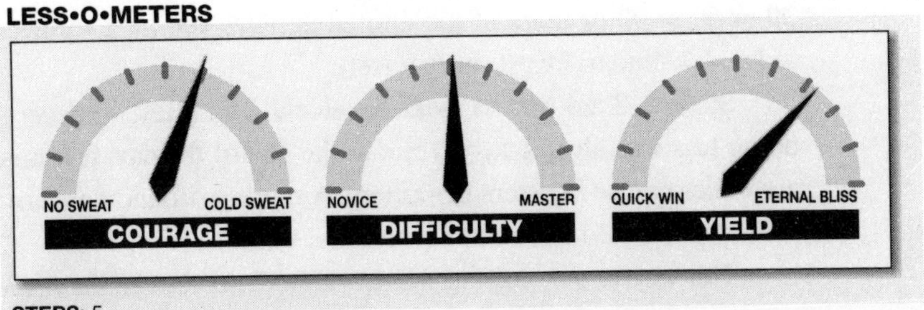

STEPS: 5

TAKEAWAY: Stop going to meetings you're *supposed to*

KEEPING SCORE: You can cut *supposed to* meetings in half!

WHY DO LESS

Meetings are probably on your list of the five least productive things you do at work.[1] • NewsFlash: Your grandchildren's grandchildren will say the same thing • This problem is not going away

HOW TO DO LESS

1

Remember one number: 1440

It should inform most every choice you make about most every meeting you attend.

1440 is the number of minutes in a day

You can't change that number, and you don't get carry-overs from one day to the next. And no matter how politically incorrect it is to cut out on wasteful meetings, or how much courage it takes not to go in the first place — if you go, you are choosing to fritter away 30 or 60 or 90 or more of the limited minutes you have to invest today. It's time to invest more wisely.

Steps 2–3 ask you to make tough choices. (Hey, whoever said doing less was always easy?) But at the end of the day, few meetings are either career-boosters or -killers. A more profound concern is "What else could I have done with that time?"

The way to stop asking that question is to change the meetings you go to in the first place.

(We'll dig deeper into 1440 in Chapter 13)

2

If you're like most everyone, you'll need to change the filter you use to choose which meetings to attend

Most of us go to meetings because we're *supposed to*. Good employees (who want to stay employed) go to all their boss's meetings. Good teammates go to all team meetings. Customer-focused employees go to every customer meeting. Only bad people, or those committing career suicide, don't go to meetings they're supposed to. Right?

Wrong.

If you go to all the meetings you're *supposed to* — including ones called by your boss or some other decision-maker — you will have no time left to get anything done. Being *good*, in the old sense, is no longer viable.

•

Ask yourself these three questions before you decide to attend any meeting:

1. **How much value will I *get* from this meeting?** (Your ROI)
2. **How much value can I *contribute* to this meeting?** (Increasing the ROI for your team, company, or customer)
3. **If I was hit by a bus that day, would the meeting happen without me?** (The ultimate litmus test. A milder version is the 100-Mile Test: If I worked a hundred miles away, is this a meeting I'd attend?)

•

Your time and attention are limited assets which bosses, teammates, customers, and family members all want more of. Every meeting request is a negotiation between you and them for those valuable assets. That's why you need to shift from blind obligation — ("I'm *supposed* to attend.") — to evaluating value, that you receive, and that you provide to others.

3

Now that you've got a new filter...

Use it!

Every day.

Get disciplined in asking those three questions

Some people rank every meeting request on a 1–5 scale. (1= Lowest possible value from attending the meeting. 5 = Highest.) If that works for you, go for it!

But that's probably extreme. There are other, simpler, ways of getting disciplined:

- **First,** know where the *majority* of your meeting invites come from. Via electronic calendaring programs? Email requests? Via phone, or at the end of previous meetings? Train your Do-Less antennae on the channel that generates the most requests for meetings. Focus on this channel above all others.

- **Next,** if you find you need a reminder, tear out those three questions from Step 2. Tape the questions where you'll see them when requests come in: On your computer, in your notebook, by your phone, etc. (The Do-Less Toolkit in the back of the book has tear-out pages for this very purpose!)
- **Finally:** Pause. Reflect. Reserve just the briefest moment to consider those questions before replying "Yes, I'll attend your meeting." (If you're on your computer or phone, you can do this by staring at the three questions as you reply. In a meeting, stare at the questions while everyone else is whipping out their calendars and Palm Pilots.)

Odds are good that you will immediately decrease the number of meetings you attend.

•

People who follow these three steps for at least one month

report a 10% to 30% reduction in meetings attended.[2]

•

After six months they

report a 30% to 50% reduction in meetings attended.[3]

❹

Use common sense

Of course, there are meetings you will *have to* attend. Of course, you need to be more careful when following these steps with superiors. We all make exceptions, even after those questions tell us not to go to the meeting!

Just be careful of Exception Creep: allowing so many exceptions that you end up going to the same number of meetings.

5

When you do go to meetings, use the CLEAR model

These five questions will help you get more *out of* any meeting:

• **Connected**	"Help me understand how this is connected to my current projects?"
• **List next steps**	"Could you list our immediate next steps?"
• **Expectations**	"What are your expectations for success? By when?"
• **Ability**	"Help me understand how we'll get everything done. What tools and support are available?"
• **Return**	"How does this help our team achieve our goals?" "How does this project move me closer to my goals?"

Bonus Tips

Avoid ALL regularly scheduled meetings

The agendas for regular monthly or — (worse) — weekly meetings tend to revolve around filling the blocked-off time. Always respond to an attendance request with "Tentative," and then wait until you see the actual agenda to decide to go or to send your regrets.

If you have the opportunity to create the agenda for other people's meetings, grab it!

Advantages include: positive dependencies (on you), enhanced ability to influence outcomes, favors owed, accomplishing your own work without having to call another damn meeting!

WHAT'S BEHIND DOING LESS

I've asked successful leaders how they decide which meetings to attend. **"Only those which produce the highest returns"** is a common reply. Their approach? "Ruthless. My time is limited. My focus and attention must be wisely invested — for customers, shareholders, and all employees," said one leader who spoke for many.

Here's an example of how that plays out: A large company recently embarked on a 20-week project to reinvent how it delivers its products. Eight teams were formed. They met once a week with assignments in between. A Core Team was established to coordinate the teams' efforts, and make progress reports to the senior executives who sponsored the project. Total meeting time with the senior team: five hours. Total hours spent by all the teams: More than 5,000. That's a 1,000:1 ratio.

At the end of the project, all 14 senior executives committed one full day to review the recommendations. And those in the Core Team marketed that day to all involved as evidence of the senior team's "true commitment to this project." When one day of face-time counts as true commitment, somebody's got tight reins on how their time gets spent!

That scenario is not atypical. Most senior execs *are* ruthless in what they allow on their calendar. The best ones do this to maintain focus on high-value activities, and create the most value for all stakeholders. Consistent focus, when all around them jump from crisis to crisis, is a skill that all great leaders possess.

I know what you're thinking — (I used to think this too): "Those leaders *can* be ruthless with their calendars and meeting time because they're the head honchos. They can say 'no' when I can't."

Not so. I've interviewed hundreds of leaders about how they manage their workload and how they spend their time. Asked when they first began to carefully manage their calendar, the most common responses, in rank-order, have been:

1. "Always. I've always been highly focused in what gets my attention."
2. "When a mentor [or development program] helped me change."
3. "When I learned the importance of focus the hard way." (Recounting a painful lesson-learned.)

Today's most admired senior execs closely managed their calendar long before they had the "authority" to do so. And tomorrow's leaders are doing the same thing today. Are you?

•

Our work is an investment

Our time and attention are finite. We choose where and when to invest our experience, knowledge, passion, and energy and how much to invest. And the social networks we use to get stuff done and the friends and teammates whose trust we have earned. Tell us again: Why should we invest all these assets in you?[4]

Those words are an amalgam based on the interviews I've done with time-conscious executives, managers, and employees rolled into one. The future of work is managing a portfolio of limited assets — like time and attention — far more wisely than most of us do today.

Being more selective about which meetings to attend is one of the first steps toward thinking like an investor.

WANT MORE?

Basic Tips

- Chapter 10: How to Say "No" to Anyone in Any Situation

Power Tips

- *The Four Agreements,* by Don Miguel Ruiz
- *The Power of Now,* by Eckhart Tolle
- *Work 2.0: Building The Future, One Employee At A Time,* by Bill Jensen

8

How to
Do Less and Still Run a Great Meeting

LESS•O•METERS

STEPS: 5

TAKEAWAY: Get the right people in the room for the right reasons

KEEPING SCORE: Meetings are life, reduced to 15-minute segments. Run them that way!

WHY DO LESS

Push the best practices you've learned to the back of your brain •

There are just too many details to master

There's only one guiding principle:

Be the example

- Put on a meeting you wish someone would invite you to
- Yes, the devil is in the details
- Yet, if you follow this principle, you'll get more of them right, and be forgiven when some go wrong

(So what follows is a drill-down into that guiding principle. If you're seeking important tips like "have an agenda" and "bring cookies," then skip this chapter entirely. Instead, go to the *Want More?* suggested readings.)

HOW TO DO LESS

Pre-Work

Remember one of the three Laws of Workplace Behavior:
Ease-of-use and reduced-use-of-time are *huge* in their ability to drive human behavior.

When you agree to sponsor or run a meeting, approach your responsibility as if you are being handed a portion of someone's life. Because you are. (Remember 1440, from page 54.)

1

Decide what the meeting's about, and who needs to attend.
There are only three types of meetings

	MEETING TYPE AND OBJECTIVES	WHO ATTENDS	LEADER'S PRIMARY PLANNING TASKS
1.	**Brainstorming: Creating New Ideas, Approaches** **Leader:** Sponsor or Champion	• Representative stakeholders • Contrarians, out-of-box thinkers • Content experts	• Get the right people in the room • Tightly articulate the meeting's objective
2.	**Connecting People and Ideas: Creating Aha's and Alignment** **Facilitator:** Usually Team Leader or Sponsor	• Whoever must take ownership of the meeting's outcome	• Get the right people in the room • Be extremely clear about success (see Step 3)
3.	**Making Decisions, Planning Next Steps** **Leader:** Final decision-maker. Usually focused on implementation needs	• Decision-makers • Representatives of those who must implement whatever is decided	• Get the right people in the room • Be extremely clear up front: Decision by consensus, or by one decision-maker? Either approach is OK. Lack of up-front clarity is not.

4. Information Sharing

This type of meeting should be completely banned. Today, there are more efficient/effective approaches. Anyone who proposes an Information Sharing meeting should be drawn-and-quartered and then boiled in oil.

2

Now, IGNORE EVERYTHING I JUST SAID about only three types of meetings

That's for the fake, on-paper, well-planned world.

In the real world, most meetings — including the best planned — are fuzzy combinations of the three types. And that's OK. The main reason you need to know the differences between them is to get this right:

> **Get the right people in the room.**
> **(Or on the phone, or online.)**

Woody Allen famously said that 80% of success is just showing up. About 80% of your success is getting the *right people* to show up. **If you get the right people in the room,** they'll help you smooth out the meeting details that go *kaflooey* or get the agenda back on track if it begins to wander.

And if you truly respect people's time, you'll bring together the **smallest possible number of people** — for the decisions that must be made and the work that must be done — instead of a running politically correct Keep-You-In-the-Loop-Lovefest like ineffective managers often do. (Send the required In-the-Loopers a CLEAR email after the meeting.)

3

Define success for your meeting

3 a

Define Behavioral Success:
What would you see and what would you hear during the meeting that would tell you it's successful?

Ask yourself the following questions beforehand:

- Who would be talking to whom? About what?
- What responses/comments would you hear if they "got it"?
- Sometimes uncomfortable discussions create breakthroughs.

What would a difficult, yet successful, conversation sound like? Look like?

- How would you know that people are tackling the right issues — how would their follow-up questions and suggestions change?
- How would you know that people were truly aligned — what would they agree to do, or not do?
- Is there anyone in the room whose changed-behaviors matter most? If so, what would you need to see or hear to confirm his/her attitudes and behaviors were changing?

People who run great meetings know what behavioral success (and failure!) look like before they begin a meeting. But they don't overcomplicate their view. They pick one or two things to listen for, and watch for.

3 b

Define Outcome Success:

What is the objective of this meeting?

- You're about to spend, collectively, x-number of valuable person-hours in a meeting. What must be accomplished by the end of the meeting — that couldn't be accomplished without bringing these people together? In Corporate Speak: What's your deliverable?

How will conversations change after this meeting?

What will people talk about, and how will they talk about it?

- People change their decisions, priorities, and actions through conversations with others. So one of your meeting's key outcomes will *always be* how conversations change afterwards.

4

Communicate Behavioral-Success and Outcome-Success up front, as you begin your meeting

Simply. In no more than three bullet points or sentences.

Can be verbally, on a flipchart, or in blinking lights on your chest.

Just be clear and succinct. (For more, refer back to Know, Feel, Do details. Oops, I mentioned it again….)

5

The most important step of all:
Show your passion

For every meeting planning detail that can go right or wrong, passion trumps them all.

Let people know how excited you'll be if you hear certain kinds of conversations and if the team accomplishes the overall objective.

Be passionate about the reason everyone's in the meeting. (And not just in the opening keynote address — throughout the entire meeting!) While the devil of meeting design is in the details, the meetings we all remember are the ones where the leader really wanted us there, and really cared about what we accomplished.

WHAT'S BEHIND DOING LESS

Meetings are life, reduced to 15-minute segments. Without the benefit of rehearsed scripts or soundtracks to let us know what to expect.

Doing them really well, and getting everything right most of the time can be complicated, difficult, and require lots of planning and experience. No matter how good your corporate culture, how clear your objective, how sharp your skills, and how great your teammates, all of humanity's vices, virtues, desires, quirks, foibles, baggage, and brilliance are invisible invitees at every meeting.

Because meetings are about people. And people bring all those things, and more, with them.

Yes, it's important to learn how to facilitate discussions, keep everyone focused, have an agenda, bring cookies (…did you know that there's a direct correlation between smile-sheet success of a meeting and how much attendees liked the food?…), ensure that the space and

technology work well, start on time, end on time, and more. The pressures to get all that right, while creating environments that inspire fun, creativity, and innovation, are so onerous that they've spawned an entire industry.

Strategy and change firm Cap Gemini Ernst & Young makes a simple promise: "We can help you make big decisions in days instead of months." To deliver on that promise, they've built Accelerated Solutions Environments (ASE). Their approach includes movable floor-to-ceiling white boards, technology for importing, displaying, and capturing electronic information, lots of toys, and inspiration libraries, all tied together with Cap Gemini's three-step acceleration change process.

ASE is an early step toward the future of meeting design, where companies will outsource all of their most important meetings, in the same way they outsource cafeteria or janitorial services. Cap Gemini has figured out that meeting design is such a critical competency that many companies will gladly pay for that service if it yields morebetterfaster results.

But most of us will be in charge of those lesser-but-still-important day-to-day meetings — where there's no outside consultant with Magic Meeting Dust to sprinkle around.

Because there's so much to master in the design and running of meetings, what you need to do is always stay focused on just one guiding principle....

•

Just be the example. Try to run your meeting like one you'd want to be invited to. **And be passionate about why people are there.**

That's it! If you focus on those two things, most everything else will fall into place — and when it doesn't, most people will forgive and forget.

We have all attended (if we're lucky) at least one mind-blowing, life-changing meeting, as well as more than our share of mind-numbing, what-am-I-doing-here time-wasters. What distinguished one from the others?

I stumbled upon an ultimate *Be the Example* experience seven years ago, and have been learning from it ever since. Once a year, there's an event that the founder calls "the dinner conversation I always wanted to have." There are no keynote speakers — everyone gets equal billing. There are presentations, but most of the time is reserved for conversations. Just like a dinner party.

This get-together was so transformational for me that, last year, I asked my fifteen year-old son to take a week off from school and join me. Among others, he had in-depth conversations with skin-publisher Christie Hefner, playwright Neil Simon, music producer Quincy Jones, and a 12-year-old film-maker. Now, at the still-young age of 16, he counts that meeting as a life-changing experience. (To learn more about this event, go to www.ted.com)

•

Other *Be the Example* meetings…

- A mid-manager, facilitating a Six Sigma meeting in a manufacturing plant, refused to make a single statement the entire meeting. She only asked questions. Boy, did that change the dynamic! The team created their own answers, and set new targets, instead of the other way around.
- At the last minute, one senior exec at a software firm threw out his scripted PowerPoint rah-rah presentation, and, instead, invited a panel of customers to come up and tell the group what they thought of the company's products. Now that was a meeting people talked about for years!
- An apparel label-manufacturing CEO did something similar: Ripped up the planned agenda, and took the 250 execs — who were attending from 38 different countries — to a local mall. They studied their product from the consumer and retailer's perspective.

- A mega-bank needed to design meetings that relayed the same content, in the same way to over 100,000 people — in a matter of days. The bank also recognized the need for deep discussion among every attendee during the meetings, and their current web-technology couldn't handle that. Solution: A pre-scripted videotaped facilitator. He'd ask a question, the screen would go blank for the allotted discussion time, then he'd pop up with another question. (Table facilitators had some fact-based handouts to further guide the discussions.) The feedback on the meetings was through-the-roof fantastic!

•

These are among the experiences that I turn to for inspiration when I get to run a meeting. You have your own experiences and sources of inspiration. Use them!

Your inspiration for *Being the Example* can be your Uncle Louie and his outrageous family get-togethers, your most wondrous experience as a student, or how your mentor ran her business meetings. Anything. As long as it comes from inside of you, and not some how-to Meeting Guide.

Because great meetings — the ones nobody wants to miss — are your life, parsed into 15-minute segments. (A little homework in those detaily things wouldn't hurt! Check out these sources for the basics….)

WANT MORE?

Basic Tips

- "50 Ways Not to Get Dinged: A Devil-in-the-Details Meeting Guide," go to www.simplerwork.com
- "The Manager's Guide to Effective Meetings," *Harvard Management Communication Letter,* Product #6315
- *The Complete Idiot's Guide to Meeting and Event Planning,* by Robin Craven
- *The Business Meetings Sourcebook,* by Eli Mina
  At 653 pages, there's gotta be something you'll find helpful!

9

How to Give Executives Less Information and Keep 'Em Happy

LESS•O•METERS

STEPS: 8

TAKEAWAY: Tell a story about control or risk

KEEPING SCORE: Turbo-charge your career! Compress the most value into the least time

WHY DO LESS

Unless your full-time job is keeping senior execs informed, you need shortcuts for getting them what they need as quickly as possible!

HOW TO DO LESS

1

Data will set you free!

ONLY if you use it to tell a story or start a tough conversation.

Do not just "present" numbers.

The budget, or sales or quality figures, or reduced costs — or whatever numbers you've been told to present — are never the real reason you've been asked to make a presentation.

Despite everything you've heard, hard-numbers, performance results, measurements, and quantifiable reasoning are only proxies for what really matters. So you shouldn't use all your available time jumping through hoops to search for and scrub numbers.

If you are asked to make a presentation to a senior executive (as opposed to an invitation for dialogue), the odds are very good that it's about one of two things:

- Control
- Minimizing the executive's personal exposure to risk

DO organize your presentation to tell a story

Focus immediately on the headline, which must always be:

- **"Boss, things are under control / not under control."**
- **"Boss, whether my news is good or bad, your butt is safe with me."**

(For more, see example)

2

Plan for one-third of the allotted time

Most execs want to "cut to the chase" far earlier than you think they should. So, plan on being interrupted almost as soon as you begin. If you've been given an hour, assume you'll only be presenting for about 20 minutes total — in increments of no more than five minutes.

Even if your senior execs don't interrupt this much, all executives *love* presenters who take *less* time than allotted! Always plan on using one-third the time you've got, and you'll receive rave reviews in any executive suite.

Turbo-charge your career! Make effective use of your exec's time and you will be known for: getting to the point, being a good thinker and clear communicator, and someone who will help executives increase their effectiveness!

❸

Reduce everything to one page

Remember the Grand Poobah Law: If it has a staple in it, it doesn't get read. Never walk into any presentation without a one-page summary (of display-size type).

❹

Focus on the past 90 days. And the next 90 days. Anything beyond that is irrelevant

You have a snowball's chance in hell of getting an executive to focus beyond 90 days. So get over it, and move on.

Be as detailed as you can about what is planned for the next 90 days. For example: If you are presenting a one-year plan in ten pages, spend nine pages on activities during the next 90 days — and one page for the rest of the year.

❺

Shop your presentation around ahead of time

Typical senior execs hate two things: 1) Surprises. 2) Spending time on anything that their lieutenants haven't already vetted. Pre-selling your presentation to the lieutenants keeps you covered on both.

Spend time with those individuals *before* you make your presentation. Allow them to meddle with wording and refocus what you have to present. For the lieutenants to take ownership of your presentation, they need to see their fingerprints all over it. (For the balancing act between their fingerprints and your personal integrity, see Chapter 24.)

If possible, everyone involved should have your presentation in their hands at least one week ahead of time.

Steps 1–5 organized your presentation. Now, let's look at what you say and do…

6

Invite them to participate quickly, before they jump in on their own

Within the first five minutes you should be asking: "Does that jibe with your experience?" or "Have I correctly portrayed success for this project?" or "Would you change how we're positioning this?" Create opportunities for the execs to express their views. Since that is going to happen anyway, plan for those moments or you will relinquish the pacing and focus of your presentation.

7

If you need something from the executive:
Be clear, direct, and succinct about what you need

They are hit with too many requests that *sound like* avoidance — pushing decisions that should be made in the middle of the organization up to the top. Mostly because the requests are not properly framed.

For example: If you want the executive to support your new product initiative, don't ask for "sponsorship" or a "champion" for the project. That sounds like you haven't done your part and are waiting for Power From Above to jumpstart your efforts. Instead, itemize everything you've already done, and then spell out specific sponsor activities during the next 30 to 60 days: how many meetings he'll have to attend, who the audience is, what messages he'll deliver, etc. Be as specific as possible, *and* as brief as possible.

8

Always have a Trojan Horse Agenda

This last step is supercritical. Never walk through the gates of the executive suite without a hidden agenda: The Search for Deeper Clarity.

Take advantage of your face-time with the leadership of your company. In most firms, much of the communication that comes down from senior execs is either (occasionally) unfocused and full of mixed messages, or (most often) has passed through so many filters before it gets to you that it no longer has any meaning.

So, regardless of whatever you have to *present* to them, always have something prepared to *ask* them. What do you want to know about the new innovation program, or how the new strategy changes your work, or how the company is going to counter what the competition just did? You have an opportunity to address the ambiguities of your job, and gain a little more clarity. Use it!

Example: Happy Execs in Ten Pages or Less

Recommendation: No more than ten pages. One to five pages is even better.

PAGE	TALKING POINTS	TIME
1 **Title Page:** "See, I'm using your jargon. I'm packaging my work by using Senior Exec phrases and themes-of-the-month."	• Be absolutely clear about the purpose of meeting, the reason for this presentation, and what you'll be asking for when you're done	**30 secs**

PAGE	TALKING POINTS	TIME
2 **"Here's everything I have to tell you, on just one page."**	• 5–6 bullet points providing an overview of your entire presentation. All but one of these points portray a reality the exec wants to see: Things are on-budget, on-time, etc. • Don't deliver spreadsheets — tell a story! Use headlines! Are you on top of things? That's what execs quickly want to know: What in your presentation will reassure them, or increase their risk-exposure when they have to present to *their* bosses? (For example: "We're On Target! $50 MM") • 1 bullet point should present a problem you want the exec to address. (If you've demonstrated that most of your presentation is about being a good soldier, and you're only presenting one challenge out of 5–6 points, they'll gladly help you problem-solve this one point.) • If you are successful, most of your time should be spent on this one page.	**15 – 30 mins** **You presenting:** 5 mins **Balance of time:** Execs questioni debating, understanding v you're presentin
3 – 9 **The numbers and details behind your one-pager**	• Offer all the numbers — pie-charts, Excel spreadsheets, etc. — behind your one-pager. • Especially given all the recent accounting scandals, you must provide excruciatingly detailed numbers to have credibility. But spreadsheets and data dumps should NEVER be the focus of your presentation. If you get sucked into a numbers-driven presentation, you've just increased your workload, while reducing the executive's. Is that how you want to work?	**10 – 15 mins**

PAGE	TALKING POINTS	TIME
10 **"Here's what we need from you, so we can succeed."**	• 3–5 bullet points providing an overview of what you need from the senior exec. Be as specific as you can (See Step 6) • This page is supercritical. If you don't focus on this, every presentation will be made in corporate purgatory: constantly making presentations, but gettin nothing out of them in return	**5 – 10 mins** **You presenting:** 2 – 5 mins **Balance of time:** Engaging senior execs in their role in your project

Reminder:

<u>Every</u> presentation should always be about creating great dialogue, not 'presenting'.

WHAT'S BEHIND DOING LESS

I have witnessed hundreds of presentations to senior executive teams. I have read thousands of those presentations. **Many fail, for three common reasons:**

- Most underlings don't understand how data are used to make decisions, and what's really important to their execs.
- Most don't use data to make a point. They data-dump, in anticipation of any and all possible questions the execs might ask
- And when they're not data-dumping, they're blabbering without nailing the key point the execs need to hear.

(See Chapter 6: The evils of PowerPoint)

•

"Gimme the summary. Get to the point. Help me make a decision, fast. Or I'll make it without you." This is what most senior execs crave. In many ways, their behavior is no different from yours or your teammates'. Like you, they are overloaded with too much clutter. Like you, their job is to figure out what's really important in all that noise. Like you, they need to make decisions quickly, and move on.

•

The Grand Poobah Law. Whether it's words, numbers, or graphics, there is power in distilling everything you have to say to one page. It focuses conversations and decisions on what really matters.

In 2003, the United States federal budget for IT expenditures was $50 billion dollars. As an associate director of the Office of Management and Budget, Mark Forman's job was making progress reports to President Bush on how that money was being spent, and how it supported the president's overall agenda on such issues as Homeland Security. Forman's presentations consisted of a single piece of paper. All progress, by every federal agency, in categories such as Human Capital and Financial Management, were displayed graphically — with red, yellow, and green traffic light indications.[1] He and President Bush could then quickly discuss what mattered most to the president.

Yes, like you, Forman had to have all the data to back up whatever he presented. But he *told a story* with color, and "dumped" only what the president needed in his follow-up questions.

•

Helpful presentations help leaders communicate to others. Once the execs make their decisions, then they have to communicate those decisions to others. That's why concise summaries and telling stories with data are so important.

Two days after taking office as Atlanta's first female mayor, Shirley Franklin had to break the news that the city faced a 2002 budget gap of $90 million. She didn't create the shortfall, but it was her problem. One year later, Atlanta had erased the deficit and created a $47 million surplus. The solutions have their downsides and detractors, but Franklin's leadership and her approach are being studied by many cities, counties, and states which are also struggling with huge shortfalls.

Part of what helped create this turnaround was Atlanta's partnership with consulting firm Bain & Co. They donated three years of assistance and boiled down reams of budget gap data and presented its essence to Franklin. In turn, she used what she learned to convince business leaders, labor leaders, the public, and even her political opponents to share the city's pain and financial burden, and to set aside departmental agendas.[2] Like Bain & Co. did for Franklin, your presentations can be used by your executives to convince others to change.

•

Bossphobia. There is a reason that suggestions in this chapter have pushed the Courage and Difficulty Less•O•Meters to their highest levels in the book so far: It's Bossphobia.

John Weaver, psychologist and coach with Psychology for Business, a Waukesha consulting firm, estimates that between 10% to 15% of people have moderate fears of dealing with their boss. And that those fears hold them back from fully pursuing their careers.[3] Those percentages are probably much higher when it comes to saying more to executives with fewer pages in a presentation.

I have no Bossphobia Magic Wand. But I can promise you that all the steps and sidebar details in this chapter are the secrets of those who have mastered the art of making presentations to their bosses.

WANT MORE?

Basic Tips

- For a sample ten-page presentation, go to www.simplerwork.com

Power Tips

- "The Power of Talk: Who Gets Heard and Why," by Deborah Tannen, *Harvard Business Review,* Article Number 9977

10

How to
Say "No" to Anyone in Any Situation

LESS•O•METERS

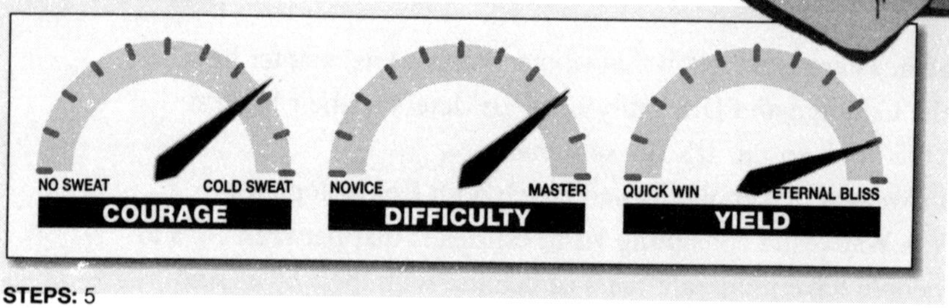

STEPS: 5

TAKEAWAY: Everyone is moving their to-do's onto your plate

KEEPING SCORE: How your response *this* time changes *future* expectations

WHY DO LESS

Either get good at frequently saying "no," or become a permanent victim of Downhill To-Do's • It's that brutally simple

HOW TO DO LESS

1

Trust your gut for the first cut.

Not your head

Often suppressed, beneath years of Pavlovian, politically correct decisions, is your gut. That inner voice — if you trust it — will tell you whether or not you're in a situation where you should be saying no.

Downhill Victims, people who take on too much that comes from above, jump too quickly into risk-analysis: "Will I commit career suicide if I say no? What will my boss, or client, or teammates think if I said no? What will I miss out on if…" This becomes a self-fulfilling prophecy. Most every time, often within seconds, they've rationalized "yes" — and added one more to-do.

So the first cut in determining which requests you'll oblige, and those you won't, comes from your gut:

•

"What do I want to do? Or not want to do? What is best for me?"

•

Begin by listening to your inner voice. Saying no more often doesn't mean taking unnecessary career risks. It's about giving your own needs a fighting chance, and not limiting your options before you've begun. (See Law•O•Less box for why this is so important.)

2

Now that you're clear on what you want to do, pick an approach: Direct or Indirect

Note: You're not yet saying "yes" or "no"…you're just selecting an approach

Direct

"No." • "No. Thank you, though." • "Too busy. I'll pass."

With Whom	• Close teammates, friends, those who know how often you say yes • People with whom you have little or no personal connection
Criteria	Social capital: The depth (or non-existence) of your relationship with this person
How Often	About 25% of all opportunities to say no
Watch For	**COMMON MISTAKES** • Over-explaining the reasons for "no," over-apologizing • Buying time: saying yes, then gently backing out later. Which does a disservice to both parties: adding unnecessary to-do's, disguised as kindness **BEST PRACTICES** • One to twenty words • Be direct sooner, you'll reduce unnecessary back-and-forth

Indirect

"Help me understand..." • "Let's talk about this..."

With Whom	• Bosses, customers, leaders; Those who direct your actions • Networked teammates: those in the same company, group, or team, but not tied to your daily routine
Criteria	How your response *this* time will create *future* expectations — yours and theirs. Take the indirect approach to manage the *overall flow* of to-do's from these individuals
How Often	About 75% of all opportunities to say no
Watch For	**COMMON MISTAKE** Trying to get rid of your *current* overload instead of educating your boss and teammates about how you want to manage their *future* handoffs to you. **BEST PRACTICES** • Focus on the relationship Incremental pushbacks over time • Find alternative solutions • Treat pushbacks as opportunities to educate th

Now that you've picked an approach...

3

Communicate Direct No's as quickly as possible, with as little thought and hesitation as possible

One to twenty words. "No thanks," and you're done!
Your best buddies will either understand or forgive you.
And while it would be nice to be nicer to those you don't know, you just don't have the time.

While Direct No's account for only a quarter of your opportunities to push back, that's where most of us spend most of our time! Because these are *comfortable no's*, low-risk, almost-fun no's.

Your goal is to spend as little time, emotion, and energy here as possible. Invest whatever you've saved into Indirect No's.

4

Treat Indirect No's as an opportunity to change a relationship, to build mutual respect

DO NOT focus on getting rid of the work you've just been handed.

In a business environment where the Number One behavior is moving To-Do's onto someone else's plate*, as soon as you directly push back on an assignment or request, you create an adversarial situation. You just increased that person's workload by pushing it back onto their plate.

*(Whether this is an acceptable or correct behavior is a another matter, for another book! Here, it's just a given — part of how work gets done.)

•

DO focus on the conversation.
Control what you can, and forget the rest.
You can change the exchange.
You can change how you react.

•

Focus on three things, always leading with questions:

- **Discover the Unsaid**

  Thanks for your confidence in me! Why'd you think of me?
  Help me understand what you're trying to achieve...
  Help me understand the connection to my quarterly goals...
  What's connected to this project that's driving the deadline?
  What would success look like for this project?
  Once I hand this back to you, what happens next?
  Even if they are minimal, what tools/support/resources are available?
  What's worked in the past?
  What do you wish you could have changed last time?
  What else is on your plate besides this project?

- **Explore Alternative Solutions**

  Ya know, Alpha Team had a problem like this... How about if we...?
  What if I presented two solutions that stayed within the budget?
  Here's how I'd start... What am I missing?
  Looking at what's already on my plate, what can I put on hold?
  Which of these three approaches do you think is best?
  Are there others who should be involved in this?
  Can I outsource this to a contractor/vendor/consultant?
  Could I set up a mid-point check-in with you?

- **Contract for the Next Conversation**

  I'll make it go away, Chief! Could we set up a debrief talk afterwards?
  To get this project done, others fell off my plate: Can you help me find a way to avoid that next time?
  I'd like to make suggestions to help do this even better next time, OK?
  I'm glad you're thrilled with how I delivered on this! — Now, can we talk about...?

If your goal is to reduce the overall flow of to-do's from someone, these three tracks of questions — **Discover, Explore, Contract** — work! Not necessarily by making any one task go away. But they deliver what you're really after:

Respect. Partnership

By asking these questions, you create opportunities to get your concerns about overload heard and discussed *in a way* that doesn't feel like you're pushing more onto that person's plate.

5

Repeat Step 4, three to five times.

Each time, once your <u>relationship with this person</u> can handle it, ratchet up your degree of pushback

•

With reasonable people, your "no" should be heard and discussed, on its merits, within two-to-three exchanges.

•

With hard-nosed and demanding bosses, customers, and teammates, if you haven't made progress on your "no's" within five-or-so exchanges, you never will.

(If that's the case, see Chapter 12: How to Deal with Bosses Who Just Don't "Get It")

WHAT'S BEHIND DOING LESS

Chapters 10–13 are so interconnected, I've placed all the *What's Behind Doing Less* and *Want More?* text at the end of Chapter 13. Here's why…

When you connect the dots between saying "no" and deflecting more, and dealing with those who don't get it, and managing your time, you are likely to find some common themes:

- You already know what you have to do.

The steps and stories in these chapters merely help you discover the courage to do what you know is right

- If you treat your daily 1440 minutes as more precious, you will remember to keep doing what you know is right, and ignore the rest
- If you follow the steps in each chapter, you'll find that you'll ask yourself more questions about why you're doing stuff. That's a good thing!
- All that newfound courage and perspective changes how others see you, and how they approach you

The Four Myths of No

1. **Saying no is a career killer.**
   The real killers are way beyond your boss's control — (like the economy or company performanc
   Now, violating someone's trust, or failing to deliver on a commitment. Those are killers!

2. **Saying yes, when we know it's silly or dysfunctional, is part of the game. We do it in the name of career advancement.**
   That quid pro quo disappeared long ago. Your boss's job is in as much jeopardy as yours. "Play the game" occasionally because you care about the people involved — because you know they'll be there for you when it counts. But not to advance your career.

3. **Staying connected with networks is important. Saying no to a teammate takes me out of the Learning/Sharing Power Loop.**
   If you adopt the Indirect approach to saying no, you will find that the new dialogue actually enhances relationships and the value you bring to the network.

4. **My boss will never accept no. I'm stuck in a no-win situation.**
   The first part may or may not be true. The second part describes a choice that you alone have made.

Laws•O•Less

The Number One behavior in business today is

moving to-do's onto someone else's plate.

The Search for a Simpler Way: By the mid-90's we began to observe a dominant workplace behavior. With hardly any exceptions, people in organizations are constantly moving as many of their To-Do's as possible onto someone else's plate. In most cases, it isn't mean-spirited or malingering, it's merely an effective way of coping with too many to-do's, too little time, and too few resources. Between 1998 and 2003, we polled over 750 individuals, asking them to rank-order the ten common workplace behaviors we observed. *Moving To-Do's Onto Someone Else's Plate* was confirmed as the behavior they encountered most often. (Of course, in follow up interviews, everyone described this behavior as "that's what others do to me. I don't do that to them." Everybody's in a circle pointing to the other guy!)

The So What? Law of Doing Less

It's fairly easy to get you to do someone else's to-do's.

Unless you learn how to push back.

11

How to
Use One Question to Do Less and Deflect More

LESS•O•METERS

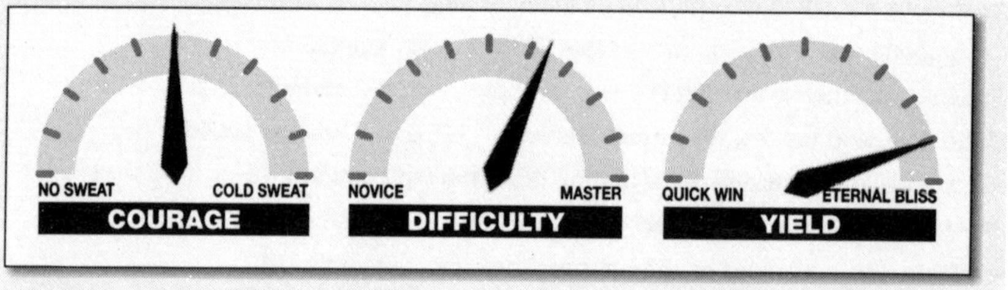

STEPS: 1

TAKEAWAY: Ask Why? three to five times

KEEPING SCORE: You've got to stop most everyone from dumping their to-do's on you!

WHY DO LESS

"Why?"

A beautiful question! • It lets you dig deep, push back, deflect, reject, and identify those who are inappropriately passing on their to-do's — while still being a helpful and caring teammate

HOW TO DO LESS

1

Ask "Why?" three to five times before agreeing to do stuff

Journalists, skilled negotiators, leaders, and counselors are taught to ask *Why? up to five times in a row.* Why? Because we humans — regardless of our role; worker, leader, parent, lover, fighter, whatever — don't dig deeply into why we do stuff, we just do it.

That may work for an impulsive romance, but when the conversation involves a boss, customer, or teammate who is asking you to take on a task for them, this very human trait can be costly. If you don't dig into why, you may be taking on unnecessary to-do's.

Getting what you need out of even well-intentioned individuals who are good communicators may take between three to five Why's to get at what they are really asking of you, or to get what you need from them to make an informed decision:

> **Boss:** *I need you to drop what you're doing, and take care of this…*
> **You:** *Why?*
> *Because the head of Alpha Team needs it by tomorrow.*
> *Why?*
> *I guess it's because they're making a presentation to the senior leadership team.*
> *Why?*
> *Because Alpha Team wants to showcase our terrific work to the senior team!*
> **Your Deflect:** *That's great! I'm happy to help out, and I'll drop everything else if that's what you want. But ya know, Marco has a presentation he made last week. Maybe we should ask him to take this on? Or at least we could do this faster, with less effort, by using his materials…*

•

Now, I know what you're thinking! I just painted the best-case scenario, where it was fairly easy to deflect a project. In the real world, your boss could have answered your third *Why?* with...

I dunno. Just do it!

...leaving little opportunity to deflect or reject.

Fair enough. Pushing back in this way will work more often with teammates and peers than it will with bosses who are in charge of your work. But there's a bigger issue here, one that changes how you listen, and how you track what's truly important...

❶ a

For all your assignments:
Ask "Why?" three to five times to discover
the full truth behind the to-do's being handed to you

You are bombarded with tons of to-do's that come from different directions — bosses, networked teammates, customers, and more — with all kinds of rationales: Because it's good for the customer... Because we need to cut costs...Because the senior team said so.

Most every reason sounds so compelling, real, or urgent, that it's easy to accept these explanations unexamined. Yet there's a different, unspoken, motivation behind many of the to-do's you are handed:

Because I'm overloaded.

This just got dumped on my plate.

And the only way I can cope is by pushing some of it onto yours.

Good people (including you) do this. We all do. It's not necessarily malicious behavior. It's just how most of us cope.

Get fanatical about asking *Why?* several times whenever you're handed a to-do. If this approach deflects only an occasional project, that's OK. The point is that you will improve your ability to distinguish between what's important and what isn't. You'll begin to see the holes in many of the rationales you're given. With that clarity, you'll gain greater confidence to say no when you encounter a request to do something that doesn't really matter.

WHAT'S BEHIND DOING LESS

See end of Chapter 13. As you connect the dots between Chapters 10 – 13, remember:

- If you don't dig into Why, you are probably taking on too many To-Do's. As well as signaling: Dump on me! Dump on me!
- They are your 1440 minutes. Don't give them up too easily

Variations of Why?

"Why?" again and again may be too much. Here are some variations.

Direct Variations For your teammates, peers	**Indirect Variations** For your bosses, customers, leaders
Why?	*Help me understand something…*
Aannnnnnnnd?	*Maybe it's me. Sorry I missed this. Could you explain…?*
Silence (…implied Why?)	*What matters most on this project?*
Tell me more…	*Is there anything I should know about how this will be used?*
	This is important because _________ (fill in blank) Right?
	Is this connected to _________ ? (fill in blank with other projects)

12

How to
Deal with Bosses Who Just "Don't Get It"

LESS•O•METERS

STEPS: 3 ways to deal with bosses; pick 1

TAKEAWAY: Pick 1 of the 3 by living according to your values

KEEPING SCORE: Moving away from, or beyond, the bozo as quickly as possible

WHY DO LESS

If your boss truly doesn't get it, he or she *never* will • So don't waste precious time, energy, and passions banging your head against a wall, trying to get this bozo to change • Instead, confirm your beliefs, and make your next career move

Pre-Work

"Getting It" Defined: Determining whether someone gets it or not isn't about whether they agree with you, or do things your way. Business is not a democracy. Hierarchies exist. So your boss has the right to make decisions with which you may disagree.

The colloquialism of "not getting it" means: not listening to reason, not weighing all sides of an issue before making a decision, being unwilling to look in the mirror, making decisions for personal gain or power instead of on the merits, etc. In a perfect world, you wouldn't have to deal with these behaviors. But the world isn't perfect, so you must. And, since none of us is perfect, you must also be certain that you haven't wrongly judged a coachable person.

•

You must be absolutely certain that you work for someone who will never get it

•

If there's a chance they may, DO NOT use the advice in this chapter. Instead, skip to Chapter 17: How to Deal with Managers Who Pile It On: MoreMoreMore, Now!

•

Here are three ways to determine whether the person above you is coachable, or will never get it. Chose one, or combine them. It's up to you…

A)

Use DISCOVER, EXPLORE, CONTRACT, in three to five different situations

- Discover the Unsaid
- Explore Alternative Solutions
- Contract for the Next Conversation (For full details, see Chapter 10)

With most reasonable bosses, it should take no more than two to three exchanges to get your issues heard and discussed on their merits. (If that's the case: this person is coachable. Skip to Chapter 17.) If your issues have not been heard and discussed within five-or-so exchanges, they will *never* be heard. (This person just doesn't get it. Stick with this chapter.)

B)

Use the AGREEMENT SPECTRUM

On any given issue, there is a spectrum of agreement. Determine where your boss falls on this spectrum:

What Your Boss Says, How S/he Behaves

COMPLETE AGREEMENT				COMPLETE DISAGREEMENT
1.	**2.**	**3.**	**4.**	**5.**
I absolutely agree with your approach, and I'm committed to it, and to you	I don't fully agree, but I trust in your wisdom, and the wisdom of the group	I'm sorry, I disagree. Here's why… But I appreciate your input. Thank you.	Just do it my way	I will stand in the way of this. I will also enlist others to stand in the way (Rarely, if ever, said openly)

Using the Agreement Spectrum: If you find most of your conversations with your boss fall between 1–3 on the Agreement Spectrum, then s/he is coachable: skip to Chapter 17. If you encounter 4 or 5 more than once (without an apology or explanation later), this bozo just doesn't get it. (Note: "Just do it" is perfectly acceptable in the heat of the moment, when everyone's crazed. However, whenever time allows — within days or weeks, not months or years — you deserve connect-the-dot explanations on most every "just do it" you get. How else are you going to learn?)

Most often, you won't hear the exact phrases above. Listen and watch for close approximations. For help in having an agreement conversation, refer to Discover, Explore, Contract, in Chapter 10.

C)

Use the calendar.

Six months, that's it.

It shouldn't take you longer than six months to determine if somebody gets it or not. Studies have shown that most new hires determine how they fit with their manager and company culture within their first six months on the job.

So if you have sincerely tried to connect with your boss for six months and nothing has worked, the odds are that s/he will never get it. Begin looking for a new and better position — immediately!

Why Pre-Work A, B, or C?

Deciding to act

Fair or not, if you've determined that your boss truly doesn't get it, you now face a decision. The goal of all Pre-Work conversations is to help you make that decision. Use the conversations to clarify the differences between you and your boss and to help define your own goals, ambitions, desires, and intentions. And to make sure that your boss understands those intentions too.

Once you've determined that your boss is

not coachable,

and you've decided to act, here's how to deal with him or her…

HOW TO DO LESS

THREE WAYS TO DEAL WITH BOSSES WHO DON'T GET IT

- **Smile and Nod**
- **Go Around or Above**
- **Let Your Departure Do the Talking**

❶ Smile and Nod

Speech bubble: "Sure boss, whatever you say."

Thought bubble: "I'll just keep doing it my way."

Behaviors and Beliefs	You've made a conscious decision to under-invest in the company because your repeated efforts to help make changes went unrewarded and unheeded
Works Best in...	• Companies with poor people policies (Some believe these firms deserve Smile and Nod behaviors) • Companies with poor accountability and performance tracking system (No way to know who's Smiling and Nodding) • Companies going through massive change, so Smile and Nodsters are camouflaged by turmoil
Upside	A saner life by riding out most every flavor-of-the month initiative and, possibly, outlasting a succession of bosses who don't get it
Downside	You haven't improved your ability to manage your career
If Done with Integrity...	You recognize that this is a personal choice, and do not play the victim. No whining, back-stabbing, complaining, or gossiping about *them.* You invest energy, instead, in positive actions, like more time with family

•

Smile and Nod: Charlie's Story

In the early 1990s, I met Charlie, the ultimate Smile and Nod character. He was in his fifties, and while new plant managers came and went, Charlie outlasted them all.

I was conducting focus groups in a company that was, and still is, globally recognized as a great place to work. (Hardly a place where one would expect to find Smile and Nod behaviors!) They were launching process reengineering, and my job was to determine how best to roll it out to the front lines. Charlie said nothing during his focus group — he wouldn't even tell me his job title — yet, most in the room seemed to defer to him.

Charlie intrigued me. I knew he had secrets about how things *really* worked in this manufacturing plant, and I made it my mission to uncover those secrets. I tagged along with him on coffee breaks and his lunch hour. I joked, nudged, teased, and offered sincere praise — all in an attempt to connect with him.

Finally, he caved. He turned to me, like someone yearning to spill his guts, but holding back because no one else cared. "You wanna know what my job really is?" he asked, in a hushed-tone. "My job is to keep every new plant manager from fucking this place up." He continued, "I say 'Yes, Sir' to everything, and then do as little of what they want as possible."

He then went on to describe — (accurately, I might add…senior execs later admitted as much) — that, while this was a great company to work for, they aggressively promoted high potential managers. Charlie's plant was a training ground, where fresh-faced MBAs would speed through, en route to someplace else. So even great plant managers — who, according to Charlie, really did care — lasted only a couple years. And twice during Charlie's tenure, less-than-great managers had focused everyone on flavor-of-the-month programs and other ways to make themselves look better to Corporate.

So Charlie's Smile and Nod approach was "this too shall pass." He wanted a job, not a career. And he discovered that even the most demanding companies have enough gaps in their systems for a few

Smile and Nodsters to safely ride out all the storms. (He recently retired with the same pension and benefits as his teammates who saluted the corporate flag every day and drank the corporate Kool-Aid.)

2 Go Around or Above

"I'd like to talk to you about a *business* decision..."

Behaviors and Beliefs	You still believe in the company and its leadership, but see your immediate boss as a barrier to doing what's right
Works Best in...	• Companies with great people policies • Companies with great senior leaders • Companies with strong accountability and performance tracking systems — focusing on best ideas, no matter where they come from
Upsides	• Finally out from under your boss's thumb • Recognition based upon merits of ideas, not politics • Doing more work that matters, less work that doesn't
Downside	NOT that the deed will go punished — your career was *already* dead-ended! Your biggest potential downside is confirmed disillusionment: Learning that leadership actually supports the boss who doesn't get it
If Done with Integrity...	You never focus on the conflict with your boss. You're always focused on the merits of decisions made, and making the business case for new decisions
	For specific conversation suggestions, see • Know, Feel, Do; Chapter 3 • Discover, Explore, Act; Chapter 10 • All of Chapter 9: making compelling presentations to senior execs

Go Around or Above: Janiece's Story

For anyone who thinks that going around one's boss is career suicide, Janiece Webb shows us how to do it — with integrity, candor, passion, in a big company with many political whirlpools, and most importantly, with continued employment!

Janiece is a senior vice president at Motorola. She was recently stuck with a boss who just didn't get it. He tried to make her accountable for more than forty yearly objectives. She knew that was way too many, but she also knew she couldn't go above or around him right away. That *would* be political suicide, nor was it the right thing to do. She felt she needed to give him a chance.

So she spent six months pushing to get those objectives reduced to the "vital few." But even after they agreed to just a few objectives, he kept asking her team to work on stuff that was off the list. So Janiece went to *his boss* to confirm that she had, indeed, selected the right objectives. She had.

In her own words: "There have been only two times in my career when I've skinned my knees. Both times were through a lack of focus and trying to be overly responsive to too many things that were expected of me. To keep your career moving, you've got to rack up points on the scoreboard — you've got to deliver results. And you can't do that if you're trying to do too much.

"My boss and I had finally negotiated a reasonable amount of objectives, and I wanted to be sure that the agreement stuck. So I sat down with his boss, as well as other executives, to ask if I had selected the best objectives to focus on. I never disparaged my boss. I didn't mention how stupid I thought it was that I had to spend six months to get to this point — I was very positive. I just wanted confirmation that I had made the right choices before I went any further.

"From then on, during every operations review, all we talked about were the vital few goals that I had selected.

"Most senior executives are in the position they're in because they can focus. If you're going to go above your boss for things like focus, prioritization, and business results, the odds are good that you'll not only succeed, but that you'll enhance your career. You get rewarded for making your boss look good, even when he isn't right…and better business results will always make him look good.

"Some bosses will use any tactic to get you to keep doing more and more. But you've got to hold on to your own internal compass as to what makes sense and what doesn't. Most often, our instincts tell us what we need to do. We just need to remember to listen to those instincts."

(More of Janiece's story, and wise counsel, can be found in Chapter 17)

3 Let Your Departure Do the Talking

Write Your Six-Months* Notice. But keep it at home.

Behaviors and Beliefs	You have determined that your boss is a barrier, and that the company is unwilling or unable to address the situation. Writing a Six Months Notice, while keeping it to yourself, is about being committed *and* being smart. (Set a goal for getting out, begin an active job search, but don't go public until it makes economic sense to do so.)
Works Best	In any company
Upsides	• A new job, with a boss and company that gets it • Doing more work that matters, less work that doesn't
Potential Downside	Self-discovery: Some discover that it's easier to complain than to take charge of a bad situation
If Done with Integrity…	* The economy and market conditions may change the *timing*, but not the *outcome*. No matter how long it takes, you have a proactive plan for getting out. In the meantime, you maintain a positive attitude and fulfill accountabilities at your current job

Going Above plus Departure Talks Louder Than Words: John's Story

For years, John Harvey dreamed of working for American Express. "I had this infatuation with them," he says. "I always had a vision of what it would be like to work there. Then they acquired the company I worked for, Thomas Cook Travel Services, and I got to join this terrific company. You could pinch me!"

John quickly rose to Senior Vice President for Global Talent, one of the top 250 people in a company of nearly 75,000 employees. He credits some of that trajectory to his willingness to always push for the best ideas, and having senior leaders who, most often, listened to those ideas. This is partly why American Express has often been voted one of the *100 Best Companies to Work For in America.*

Suddenly, for John, everything changed.

In his own words: "My new boss had a different idea about where the business needed to go, and what was necessary to get there. She believed that maintaining the status quo was a strategy, and I couldn't support just standing still. I believed that my area, which included training, needed new direction. But instead of a frank conversation, where we could discuss our differences, she shut down. I was just wrong, and no discussion was needed.

"Within a few months, I began to realize that we would always be at odds. I used the next couple months to see if things might change but, after many tries, decided that they wouldn't.

"I had lots of conversations with other senior leaders in the company, and found that she sometimes misrepresented [American Express CEO] Ken Chenault's intentions, in order to further her own agenda. Like when the economy began to suffer in 2001, Ken made a practical move — asking us to eliminate all non-critical spending. But my boss translated this to me as *'Stop all training.'* She wanted to bring him *zero* budget expenditures, even though I found out later that's not what he asked for. He wanted thoughtful reductions that would still ensure our employees could be successful.

"After mentioning a conversation I had with our CFO to confirm Ken's intent, she lost it: 'You have no ____ing way of knowing what the man in the corner is thinking,' she said. At that point, I knew my time at Amex was coming to an end."

•

The tough conversations created clarity. "Sure, I could have tolerated my situation with her for another year or more. But all these conversations helped me see that it wasn't worth it. The question became: How much are you willing to compromise for financial reasons? Or for a company — any company? Once you get clear on your own intentionality, there is no good or bad, or right or wrong answer. Yet, for me, that clarity opened completely new possibilities that I hadn't explored before.

"I'm now enjoying my family more than ever. I'm the new owner of a fish market; I've started a network for others who are in career transition; and my antique post-card collection is moving from passionate hobby to a small business. None of that would have been possible had I stuck it out at Amex. Still, going through it all did hurt. It took me several months after my departure to say the words, 'I was fired.'"

John concludes: "Every meeting I had during those final months gave me greater clarity about my own intentions. One of my proudest moments came when my boss announced my departure on a teleconference. She said to my worldwide team of over 300 employees, '*John and I* have decided that the best thing is for him to leave. *We* have decided…'

"I interrupted her and said, 'It's really important that everyone understands that this was not my decision at all. I think I could still add value. I would have liked to have stayed and finished what I started.' It was important to me that my employees understood that I would never have asked them to follow me on an adventure, and then abandoned them midway."

An important choice. I have spoken with some of the 300 people on that call. They told me that John's departure — not his words, but how he lived his values — spoke volumes to every person on the call. They each said that John was trying to get them to be strategic business partners, while his boss wanted them to churn out transactions that would have little impact on the bottom line. Several credit him for giving them the courage to think and act differently.

For those who wish to talk back, *and* keep their jobs, John's convictions serve as a roadmap: "We all have to answer the question: Have my decisions led to a good life? Not: What regrets do I have? We'll all have some regrets. But in the end, are the regrets about the important things in life? For some, not losing their job may be what's important. That's okay. For others, *keeping* it may be their biggest regret."

WHAT'S BEHIND DOING LESS

See end of Chapter 13. As you connect the dots between Chapters 10 – 13, remember:

- Dealing with bosses who don't get it may be one of your biggest challenges. Not because it takes courage to confront your boss. But because it takes courage to admit that it's your decision to make, not your boss's. You are in charge of what happens next.

13

How to
Never Again Need a Time Management Course

LESS•O•METERS

STEPS: 1

TAKEAWAY: Become a Pushback Zealot. Now!

KEEPING SCORE: Get what you want and what you deserve. Say no more often

WHY DO LESS

Can you list your top five time-wasters? • Did you know that *none* of them can be solved with better analyzing, juggling, prioritizing, or other such nonsense? • And that four of the five can be addressed with these words…

No... Whoa...Why?

• Your ability to manage how your time is spent is directly related to your ability to push back, question, and say no

HOW TO DO LESS

Pre-Work

Time Management in the Real World: Your World

Just before midnight December 16, 2002, Amazon.com sent its business customers an announcement: A Harvard module on Time Management is available — come and get it. By the next morning, it was Amazon's Number Two seller! Important problem, eh?

The authors list their three phases of effective time management: 1) Analysis, 2) Planning, 3) Follow-up and Evaluation. They then provide a handbook for following this rigorous and disciplined approach. In other words, they want you to do the stuff you'd be doing if you had the time to manage your time in the first place!

We hear the same mantra for managing our homes and workspaces. In *Organizing from the Inside Out*, author Julie Morgenstern uses similar methods to whip our living spaces and offices into shape: analyze, strategize, attack.

Maybe supreme analytical thinking works for beating an office chair into submission, but it's completely useless against your worst timebandits.

•

Can You List Your Five Biggest Time-Wasters?

I can. Since 1992, as part of our study, *The Search for a Simpler Way*, we've asked more than 5,000 people to rank-order their biggest time-wasters. So I can say with great confidence that the biggest black holes in your workday are probably:

1. Meetings
2. Dealing with communication from others
3. Communicating to others
4. Your boss micromanaging or undervaluing you
5. Worktools and processes designed for company success, but not necessarily yours

(Your own list may switch their order. The list for very senior executives is obviously different.)

•

These five are more than petty annoyances. Consistently, I have found that the top three time-wasters — all activities relating to communication — **cost people at least two wasted hours per day!** Non-replaceable hours, gone. And problems with your boss can't be solved with time management techniques. This issue is all about your relationship with your boss, and how you deal with it. (Timebandit Five, the horrendous state of complexity built into your worktools and work environment, is another matter altogether: it's addressed in Chapter 28.)

Even more important than the list is what interviewees said would fix most of these problems. In hindsight, their two biggest responses were:

- "I should have pushed back harder, or said 'no' more often."
- "I should have questioned more. Or had better conversations with my boss."

I have found that there are two kinds of people who have pushed past "I should have…" and *are* gaining greater control over how their time is spent…Pushback Zealots: those who habitually push back, asking why to-do's deserve their attention….and…Insulated Bosses: those who shield themselves from everyday problems.

Real-World Time Management

The Two Biggest Success Stories

PROFILE	COMMON MOTIVATIONS	STRATEGIES
PushBack Zealot	• A major health, stress, or family crisis forced an immediate and urgent change • Passionate dedication to a personal mission and set of values	• Habitual in pushing back • Continually ask: "Why does this deserve my time and attention?"
Insulated Boss	"I'm important. I do important things. To get to me, you'll have to go through my assistant's assistant..."	• Gatekeepers • Lieutenants • Structures, procedures, policies • Support peons

Obviously, I cannot endorse the second of these approaches. (But I can't say it doesn't work either. Insulated bosses have excellent control over how little of their time gets wasted!) Which leads us to the one proven time management technique for the rest of us — people with real-world problems and real-world integrity…

HOW TO DO LESS AND GAIN GREATER CONTROL OVER HOW YOUR TIME IS SPENT

❶

Become a PushBack Zealot.

Now

Say "no" more often.	(Chapter 10)
Question more often.	(Chapter 11)
Call Time Out and Whoa more often.	(Chapter 12)
Just do it.	(Chapter 13)

WHAT'S BEHIND DOING LESS

Chapters 10 – 13

"They talked, and I listened.... They talked about a search for daily meaning as well as daily bread. For recognition as well as cash. For astonishment, rather than torpor. In short, for a sort of Monday through Friday life rather than a Monday through Friday void. Perhaps immortality was part of that quest. To be remembered is their wish.

"I was consistently astonished by the extraordinary dreams of ordinary people. No matter how beguiling the times, no matter how dissembling the official language, those we call ordinary are aware of a sense of personal worth, or more often, the lack of it, in the work they do. As Nora Watson said, most of us have jobs that are too small for our spirit."[1]

Those are the words of the amazing Pulitzer Prize–winning author, Studs Terkel, talking about his 1974 book, *Working*, in which he chronicled how we worked, and what we dreamt.

In my own research, beginning almost two decades later and continuing past the thirtieth anniversary of the publication of *Working*, I can assure you that our dreams remain unchanged. Most everyone I meet is on a quest for meaning, and seeking work equal to the size of their spirit, energy, and passions. That part of my job is exhilarating!

Unfortunately, I'm also finding increased hopelessness, fear, cynicism, tension, skepticism, resignation, and anxiety. More and more interviewees are reluctant to take any risks at all, or push back on stupidity and dysfunction, or say no to too many to-do's in the name of those dreams. During troubled economic times, people worry that those kind of pushbacks aren't wise at best, and at worse, could threaten one's livelihood.

•

No's, Pushbacks, and Questioning: The Bottom Line

The Simplicity Survival Handbook is a collection of best practices for doing less. Yet I know that if you are filled with anxiety and hesitation, no book, no checklist, no research finding will convince you to risk pushing back. That courage has to come from within.

Chapters 10 – 13 represent the most difficult and most courageous how-to's in the entire book. That's what makes them the most important. You are being asked, in the name of doing less, to ask yourself:

- What really matters?
- What is the price I'm willing to pay for what matters?
- What refusals have I been postponing?
- What is the crossroad at which I find myself at this point in my life/work?
- What answer would set me free?

These are not easy questions. Nor are they original to me. They come from Peter Block's wonderful book, *The Answer to How Is Yes*. In it, he captures the challenge laid before you in the chapters you've just read. He says, "The devil is not the behavior of the boss, it's the denial of our own power and the expectation that someone else will lead us to a better tomorrow."

He also hints at the solution: "The rush to a How answer runs the risk of skipping the profound question: Is this worth doing?"

Is the work you do worth doing? Is it worth it to you to push back? Only you know the answers for your situation. Here's how others have answered those questions:

- **100%** of the leaders we admire are PushBack Zealots
- **100%** of our coworkers who are truly happy are Pushback Zealots

That's the bottom line.

QUOTE OF NOTE

The most difficult task in life Is changing yourself.
NELSON MANDELA

•

Rogue's Gallery:
Portraits of Some PushBack Zealots

John Harvey (page 99) is a highly respected leader. Possibly more so after his departure from American Express. Scores of ex-teammates stay in regular contact, seek his mentoring, and have volunteered their talents to his Career Transition Network, a support community for those who are unexpectedly out of work. John is the kind of leader many of us want to be when we grow up! And he's as happy as he's ever been in his career.

•

Rest assured, you don't have to lose your job if you become a PushBack Zealot. During 2003, Challis Lowe was one of only two African-American women among the highest-paid officers at 429 big companies surveyed by Catalyst, a women's research and advocacy group. (Vital Stats: She's 57, made $740,000 in 2002, and is an executive vice president for Ryder System, a trucking and logistics firm.) In 1977, she was making just over $25,000 as a middle manager in a bank. Her main career lesson? Take risks! "I've never let being scared stop me from doing something. Just because you haven't done it before doesn't mean you shouldn't try. You have to get out of your comfort zone if you're going to progress."[2]

•

Jon Mooney did not learn to read until he was twelve years old. Now in his early twenties, he's graduated from Brown University at the top of his class, is the recipient of the distinguished Truman Fellowship for graduate study in the field of learning disabilities, and is co-author of *Learning Outside the Lines*, a guide for students with learning disabilities. Jon credits his mom for all his success. She was his Pushback Zealot: "Every Friday, she'd be in the principal's office, sometimes cursing like a truck-driver, demanding, 'You're not going to do this to Jon! Let's get him the help he needs.'" Having learned from his mom, he shares his own Zealot's advice: "Don't let a culture of experts take your power away. You are not broken. Connect to your passions. Start a fire. Plant a seed. Challenge the system."[3]

•

You don't necessarily have to buck the system to push back.

Smiling and Nodding may not be appropriate for everyone, but I have to admit that I admire Charlie (page 94). He pushed back by avoiding and sidestepping work that he felt was unnecessary, silly, short-sighted, or the product of chest-thumping by people above him. He stayed true to himself through decades of changes, dozens of managers trying to get him to do stuff he didn't want to, and scores of flavor-of-the-month initiatives.

Scott, a low-level manager at another firm, has a similar guiding philosophy. Like a lot of people, he just wants a job, not a career. Scott's motto: *Entered Unnoticed. Left Unscathed.*

Charlie and Scott have a completely different philosophy about work than John Harvey or Challis Lowe or, possibly, you. And that's OK. What's important is that they've chosen their own path, and refused to be victims.

•

C. William Jones is mad as hell, and he's not gonna take it anymore. He retired from Nynex in 1990 with a plaque, a farewell bash, and a secure pension. Or so he thought. His ex-employer, like many companies today, sees retirees as a cost-center — a line of expenses that must be cut. Pension and health-benefit takeaways are appearing in record numbers. So Jones now heads the 90,000-member Association of BellTel Retirees, one of many new organizations disgusted by corporate greed and outraged by the takeaways. What's interesting is that the very skills these retirees learned as executives are now being leveraged against brethren. "It's not unions saying this to executives," says Karen Friedman from the Pension Rights Center. "These are people who used to be them."[4]

[" "]

QUOTE OF NOTE

The hottest places in hell are reserved for those who, in time of great moral crisis, maintain their neutrality.
DANTE

•

Dan Sullivan is founder of Strategic Coach. He teaches people how *not* to work. His clients are successful entrepreneurs who don't need to be motivated to change. "Their biggest problem," he says, "is complexity. They have too much going on in their lives." Sullivan continues: "Of the 365 days a year, there are only going to be three different kinds of days…

- Focus Days, when you're producing the really best results
- Free Days, when you're rejuvenating
- Buffer Days, when you are preparing – handling the backstage of your work."[5] 95% of his clients report that they increased their income, and 89% have increased their Free Days.

Saying no and pushing back is absolutely essential if you are going to create your own Free Days and Buffer Days. The found-time comes out of your Rat Race Days.

Yet pushing back isn't a license to practice road rage. How we deliver pushbacks, how we listen, and the rules of fair play are also extremely important. With the freedom to push back comes the responsibility to do it with care and understanding.

Bill Gross is Chairman and CEO of Idealab!, a dot-com incubator that has survived the bubble's burst. He's pushing back on entire markets, redefining how companies and industries are built. Yet what was his key influence? "The Caltech Honor System [California Institute of Technology]. I arrived at college and found this crazy thing they had, where you could take all your tests in your room, there was never any proctoring, there were no locks on the doors, and there was one simple rule: no student shall take unfair advantage of any other member of the Caltech community. It had a big effect on me. I found out how much could be achieved with smart, honest, dedicated people and with teamwork. It affected everything I've done in business, and in life."[6]

•

No Easy Answers, But Common Solutions

I've met thousands of people who are just like you, who have found ways to say no more often, push back more often, and do less of what doesn't matter. *Not a single one said it was easy.* But they all have these things in common. They…

- Look inward, with no expectation that someone else will do the hard work
- Continually ask: What really matters?
- Then ask: What price am I willing to pay for what matters?
- Build support groups, seek mentors, and ask friends for help
- Rely faithfully on a personal set of values — such as trust, caring, integrity, and fairness — and will not compromise those values

In her August 15, 2001, memo, Sherron Watkins wrote: "I am incredibly nervous that we will implode in a wave of accounting scandals." Although her warnings were not heeded, she made every effort to get top execs to address Enron's deceptive practices. You know the rest: Enron collapsed, and Watkins made the cover of *Time* Magazine as Person of the Year for her whistle-blowing efforts. Says she, "I wasn't going to be able to live with myself, just slink off and find another job. I felt I had to say something and I had to do something." The courage to push back came from inside, from personal values.

[" "]

QUOTE OF NOTE

Things which matter most should never be at the mercy of things which matter least.

JOHANN WOLFGANG VON GOETHE

What isn't as widely known is that a mentor in a previous job helped her to stand up for herself more often. At Arthur Anderson, she believed she should be fast-tracked to a manager position, blowing past the standard five-year pace they insisted she follow. Her mentor's advice about the shortened timeframe: "You have to let it be known…that you deserve it."[7]

•

Starting now, let everyone know what you want, and what you deserve, and what you don't want, and don't deserve.

Say no more often.

Question more often.

Call Time Out and Whoa more often.

WANT MORE?

Basic Tips

- Take Back Your Time Day
  An initiative about the epidemic of overwork and time famine that threatens our health, our families, and our communities
  www.timeday.org

Power Tips

- The New Work Contract: Work 2.0
  www.simplerwork.com
- *The Answer to How Is Yes,* by Peter Block
- *Crucial Conversations: Tools for Talking When Stakes are High,* by Kerry Patterson, et al.
- *Fierce Conversations: Achieving Success at Work & in Life, One Conversation at a Time,* by Susan Scott
- *When You Say Yes But Mean No,* by Leslie Perlow

2

Career Milestones

Do less...

Accomp

ish more.

Your Workplace: From Entry...

.to Exit

14

How to

Figure Out If Your New Employer Will Work You Harder, Not Smarter

LESS•O•METERS

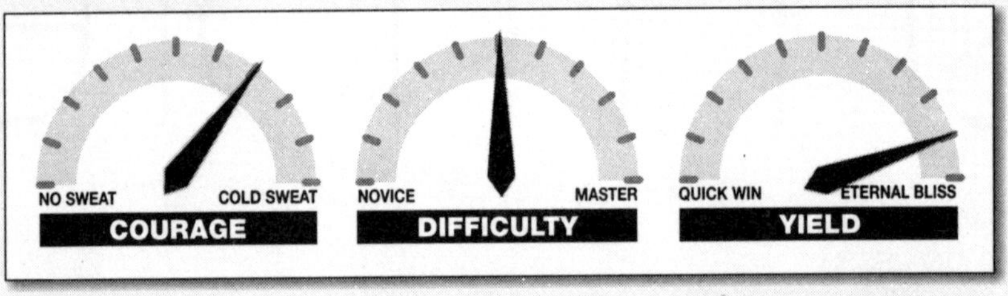

STEPS: 6

TAKEAWAY: Spend a day with your prospective employer, watching how they work

KEEPING SCORE: In just one day, you can know how hard or easy they'll make your work

WHY DO LESS

Wouldn't it be great if — *before* you took your next job, instead of months later — you could figure out whether this company makes it hard or easy to get stuff done? • You not only can fast-forward like this — you must!

Pre-Work

Here, we focus on a specific slice of interviewing for a job — quickly uncovering an employer's true views about work and how you will be expected to get everything done. This could save you months of trying to figure it out on the job, *after* you've been hired. Yet, by narrowing the focus, a lot was left out....

•

Need tips and techniques for wowing your interviewer?
Then get a copy of John Kador's book, *201 Best Questions to Ask on Your Interview*, as well as *Ask the Headhunter* by Nick Corcodilos... Great books!

It's OK to go to other resources first. We'll wait...

(...Welcome back!)

HOW TO DO LESS

❶

You've just completed your first or second interview.

They love you!

(Of course.)

Now: Ask to live a day at their place

You want a day to experience how work gets done at this company — not just hear about it in interviews. (If you're currently employed, call in sick or take a vacation day. This step is that important.)

❷ a

If the interviewer refuses, or is befuddled by your request:

Warning!!! Alarm bells!

Getting work done at this company will probably NOT be easy

The interview process is the first of many business processes you will encounter at this company. And if this firm is like most, all their processes have been designed to maximize *the company's* effectiveness, not necessarily yours. (A pattern of focusing on organizational effectiveness more often than yours will be one of the five biggest wastes of your time in this company — making it harder for you to get stuff done.)

If your interviewer refuses or is confused by your request, there is a lack of flexibility in the company's processes that will probably haunt you throughout your employment there. If you join this company, the odds are good that a lot of your time and attention will be spent accommodating their way of doing things, with little or no room for them to accommodate your needs. You may wish to reconsider whether this is the employer for you.

2 b

If their response is, "Sure! When?"
you could be looking at a winner!
Onto Step 3…

3

Ask to sit in on two or three of the following activities
during the day that you spend at the company...
(Focus on the activities that are most relevant to your new job. Offer to sign a non-disclosure agreement for anything you may see and hear.)

- Team brainstorming session (within your own department)
- Daily, weekly, or monthly team meeting where assignments are handed out
- Presentation from a senior executive to mid-managers
- Customer sales meeting
- Customer problem-solving (face to face, on the phone, or online)
- Mid-managers designing a presentation to give to senior execs
- Mid-managers evaluating some directive from Corporate
- Front-line employees meeting to discuss some directive from mid-managers

- The rollout of some big change or training effort
- Six Sigma, quality, or operations review meeting
- Quarterly, monthly, or weekly progress review meeting
- Exit interview for someone who is voluntarily leaving the company
- Interview of a prospective vendor or consultant to the company

During your day at this company you will, of course, meet with and interview your prospective manager and teammates. But you also want to go beyond those exchanges into witnessing, first-hand **how this company makes decisions, how they assign work, how they problem-solve, and how they use bottom-up ideas and feedback.**

4

Keep a record of your observations.

Rank them using the following three criteria:

(You can do this by gut. But 1–10 will likely clarify what your gut is telling you.)

	1 • • •	5 • • • •	10
1. How close a match between how this company gets stuff done and how I'd like to work	Wow! This is my kind of place!	Different. But I could learn a lot here	Help! I'm suffocating Get me out
2. How their resources matched their expectations	• Enough people • Enough time • Enough tools/support • Enough preparation beforehand	I wish I saw more resources, but it wasn't unreasonable	Whoa! We're talking Dark Ages: gerbils on treadmills
3. How their communication changed when meeting with, or talking about, their senior execs	No change whatsoever. Same level of respect, teamwork, trust, fun, focus, and accountability	Some genuflecting to the senior execs, but nothing that made me uncomfortable	Sir! Yes, sir! How high must I jump, sir?

If your rankings are between 1–5, this company is trying to make it easy to do good work.

- **Close match to the way you like to work =** Either a great fit just for you, or an indication that the company is flexible in how it applies its processes
- **Close match between their resources and their expectations =** While every company is trying to do more with less, this one is realistic about what it will take to do good work, and is very focused with whatever resources it does have
- **Close match between how junior and senior people are treated =** This company is truly focused on the work itself, and tries to minimize jumping through hoops to please its senior execs. (Communication patterns are an early warning of these types of behaviors.)

If you rank anything a 1 or 2, take whatever job they offer, quickly! This is a great place to work. However, the closer your rankings get to 5, the more *average* the company becomes — not making it hard to get things done, but not very successful in making it easy, either.

Rankings of 6–10: You already know that you should not be taking this job. But if you do, don't complain about how hard it is to get stuff done. You were forewarned.

5

Validate your observations

Have a cup of coffee with the people who were part of those activities. Ask them if what you observed was typical of what goes on in this company. Then ask them:

- *How do you prefer to work? Can you do that here?*
- *Would you change how projects are handed to you? How so?*
- *Tell me about your boss. And your boss's boss.*
- *What about this place frustrates you?*
- *What's the one thing that worries you the most?*
- *What gives you the greatest satisfaction about working here?*

6

Make a decision

Within one day, you now have a snapshot of what it's really like to work in this company. Has your enthusiasm been heightened, squashed, or tempered by this reality-check? Whatever your answer, this is a fairly accurate representation of what you would have figured out six months into your job.

WHAT'S BEHIND DOING LESS

"The biggest problems we see are **mismatched expectations** — where the candidate thought they were entering into one kind of relationship, and the employer held different views," says Sam Dobrow, president of ThoughtForce International, a Georgia-based recruiting and HR firm.

"To avoid this problem," he says, "we advise candidates to probe deeply, and make sure employers are comfortable providing concrete examples of what they will encounter on the job." That's more than sound advice. It is crucial that you dig as deeply as you can before you consider signing up with a firm.

Many studies have been done on what it costs the *employer* if they select the wrong candidate: anywhere from $50,000 in lost time, salary, and costs for a junior person to $500,000-and-up for more senior talent. Yet who is studying what it costs *you* if you choose the wrong employer — in lost opportunities, time, skill-building, career advancement, and in increased stress, frustration, and doubt?

Answer: You. And only you.

Even in a tough economy, you can not afford to spend months or years on a new job only to discover it's not the place for you. You need to know exactly what you're getting into. You need to figure out your prospective employer's views on work *before* you sign on!

•

The rules of the game have changed.

So too must you.

Is your mind filled with "yeah, buts" and concern about turning the tables on your employer, and interviewing them? Get over it.

Do you think you can avoid this day-long fieldtrip, and learn what you need by asking just the right questions? Forget it.

Employers are changing the rules of the hiring game, and you need to adapt. Quickly. The best firms are moving away from standard interviews — where you sit down and chat with one or more people — to behavioral-based interviews, where they watch how you react to a given situation. These are called **situational interviews**, and they test a lot more than what you know, or what you've done in the past. They **test who you are**.

For example: Let's say you're applying to be the manager for a retail store. You are greeted by two people, role-playing the parts of customer and cashier. The customer has a complaint that could cost the store a lot of money and create a major liability. Yet the cashier properly followed the company's policies. Through their argument (they're yelling at each other), you discover that the company's policy isn't very clear. Both parties could be right. What would you do? Quickly! This is in real-time.

While this situation plays out, your "interviewers" are on the sidelines, watching your body language, how you gather information, how you problem-solve, how you treat people, how you deal with conflict, and much more.

Hundreds of firms from General Electric to JP Morgan Chase are using situational interviews and they are setting new standards for all employers. They believe that this approach to evaluating future employees provides the best predictor of what candidates would do in real work situations.

INTERVIEW APPROACH		ACCURACY IN PREDICTING PERFORMANCE
Standard Interview	Sit-down with a manager or Personnel	**7%**
Resume Analysis	Computerized resume sifting	**37%**
Work Sample Test	Pen-and-paper skills test	**44%**
Assessment Center	Lengthy personality and skills workup	**44%**
Situational Interview	Candidates role-play in mock scenarios	**54%**

Source: *Handbook of Industrial and Organizational Psychology*

•

What this means to you

Well, if you have always been good at hiding your flaws during standard interviews, the jig is up.

On the flipside, **who said situational interviews only go one way?** Why should you be stuck with an interview approach, which is only 7% accurate in predicting who a company is, and how their work actually gets done? (See table.) Don't you want a more accurate assessment?

•

The steps described in this chapter are your own Situational Interview Toolkit. Now, of course, you'll never get managers and senior execs to perform a role-play for you! But you can observe ready-made situations that are rife with information, if you know what to watch for.

At your last job, were you bothered by how poorly your manager organized projects? Then ask to sit in on your prospective team's weekly meeting where assignments are handed out. (You'll be able to compare and contrast workflow, prioritization, and the manager's people skills.) Do you want to learn how the company really values people? Then ask to sit in on an exit interview of someone who's leaving voluntarily. (You'll hear raves or rants that the company may have otherwise buried.) Are you a mid-manager who disliked how your past employer used consultants to drive flavor-of-the-month programs throughout the company? Then ask to sit in on an interview of a prospective consultant. (You'll see whether this employer pushes back on the consultant to get grounded in the real-world needs of its employees.) Are you concerned about diversity among teammates or decision-makers? Then be sure you sit in on frontline, mid-level, and senior meetings, and observe how the diversity mix changes. All of these activities provide clues as to what you'd otherwise have to wait months to see.

I'm sure you can now brainstorm a lot more situations than I listed in Step 3. Do so. Pick the situations that will give you the best snapshots of your prospective employer's true views of work. Then enjoy your first unofficial day on the job!

WANT MORE?

Basic Tips

- *201 Best Questions to Ask On Your Interview,* by John Kador
- *Ask the Headhunter: Reinventing the Interview to Win the Job,* by Nick Corcodilos
- DDI (Development Dimensions International) White Paper: "Selection: The Validity of Behaviorally Based Interviews" www.ddiworld.com

THE WAY OUT: **EXECUTIVE COUNTER-MOVES**

Raise the Bar, Set the Standard

If you're a senior executive, and want to attract and retain the best talent:

- **Demand that HR establish a process** for "reverse" situational interviews, where candidates get to evaluate you on the criteria listed in Step 4
- **Make sure that HR solicits, and passes on to you,** how candidates ranked your company (1–10) according to that criteria

Jane Harper, IBM's Director of University Talent Programs for IBM, is an early convert to this approach: "I thought I was in tune with the expectations people have of their leaders and the companies they work for. Now, it's like, 'What was I thinking?' The best-of-the-best want to know, *before* they come on board, that they can do their best in your company. As leaders, shame on us if we're not ready to fight for talent in new ways."

Entrepreneurs: Big Returns on a Small Investment

If you run a small company, you too can get huge returns by asking candidates to live a day at your place.

Mary Ann Allison is a best-selling author, and head of the Allison Group, which consults on organizational effectiveness. While they work on large-scale projects all over the world, headcount is small and every new hire is crucial. Says Mary Ann: "We offer people we're hiring a chance to work here for a day (paid, of course) — it's good for the employer too. We just had a candidate bail when we asked him to do the sample day. He said that spending a day with us really helped him get past the stars in his eyes, and think about the details of the job. We're much happier that he bailed now rather than later. Him too."

15

How to

Get the Orientation You Deserve

LESS•O•METERS

STEPS: 4

TAKEAWAY: Ask for homework, names, and a two-way review

KEEPING SCORE: You should be in charge of your orientation, not your company

WHY DO LESS

Most orientations focus on the company's needs, not yours • Three out of every four new hires are utterly dissatisfied • Don't wait for your prospective employer to "get it"

Pre-Work

Your overall goals for orientation should be:

- Just-in-time learning: Focus mostly on what you can apply quickly
- Learn as much as you can from people and on-the-job experiences, and as little as possible from policies and formal indoctrination

DEVILISH  **DETAILS**

What Needs to Change

76% of *Search for a Simpler Way* respondents were dissatisfied or highly dissatisfied with their new hire orientation. In rank order, here's what they wanted instead…

1. **Far less indoctrination in the Company Way and company policies**
   "If I can't figure out the Company Way from the people around me, then you've got a problem."
   "Values and company-wide responsibilities should fit on one page, and unless you're telling me about life and death safety issues, all other information can wait until I feel I need it."

2. **A lot more clarity on departmental and personal goals**
   "I'm on the job six months and I still can't see a consistent focus."

3. **A lot more mentoring and networking**
   "All work, everywhere, gets accomplished by connecting with the right people."

4. **Getting me what I need to do my work**
   "Five weeks, and I still don't have a laptop. Geez."

5. **Holding my manager accountable for the success of my orientation**
   "Whatever's important here gets measured. I guess my orientation wasn't important."

Surveys: 1997–2003, 987 respondents from over 450 companies.
However, of the 98 respondents who were senior executives, almost 70% of them were satisfied or highly satisfied.
Hmmmmm. Makes you wonder.

HOW TO DO LESS

1

Before you accept a job offer,
ask about the company's new-hire orientation.
If you don't hear these three things,*
ask for them:

• Homework • 20 Names • Two-Way Review After Three Months

Before we go into what each of these entails, here's what to **AVOID**: Since there is a three-out-of-four chance (76%) that you will either get no orientation or one that does not meet your needs, do whatever you can to wiggle out of their standard approach to welcoming people into the company. Odds are it will offer a lot of what you don't need, and little of what you do.

(For Wiggling Out strategies, see Chapters 7, 10, 11, 12)

* (If these three **are already included** in your orientation, you've picked a great company that's focused on helping you do less to accomplish more! Congratulations.)

2

Ask for homework to study between the accepted offer
and your start date.
You want two or three of the following

(select those most relevant to your job):

- Your department's past three months goals and performance
- Your department's three biggest projects in the past three months
- Your department's goals and objectives for the next three months
- Your department's most recent quarterly review
- Your company's most recent quarterly review
- Your company's current strategic plan
- Your manager's yearly goals
- Customer satisfaction reports for the past three months
- Sales reports for the past three months, plus projections for the next three

- Any company-wide communication from the CEO in the past three months
- The most recent cost-cutting initiative
- The most recent innovation initiative
- The most recent department-wide training initiative
- The most recent proposal your department made to senior management

2 a

Ask to meet with your manager on your very first day to review what you have learned from your homework

Use this meeting to clarify your understanding of your department's goals and challenges, as well as having the first (of many) conversations about your own performance plan.

3

Ask for the names of twenty people you should talk to during your first month on the job

If you work in a large company, make sure at least half of these names are outside of your department. If you work for a small company, some of the people on the list may be outside of the firm. A starter kit for thinking about who these people should be:

- Key decision-makers whom influence your work
- Day-to-Day Hubs: Those who everybody seems to turn to
- Networkers: Those whose connections seem limitless
- Gatekeepers: From admin's to execs — those who provide/deny access to others
- Content Experts: Those who know the most on a given topic
- Gadflies: Those who are outspoken, and push back on the status quo
- Your manager's boss
- Best customers
- Worst customers
- Internal alliance partners
- External alliance partners

When networking with your list of twenty, play Six Degrees of Separation. Ask each one, "Who else should I be talking to?"

❸ a

When you meet with your manager on your first day, negotiate to spend time with these twenty people during your first month

If s/he refuses, you may have chosen the wrong company! Before making that call, go to Plan B: Arrange to meet these people on lunch breaks, before work and after work. Make the time. (These connections will be invaluable both helping you focus on what's important, and teaching you all the informal shortcuts.)

Your First 100 Days

A panel of 45 fast-rising stars from 35 companies, who cited their first few months on their job as key to their success, offer this list:

1. **Network, network, network**
   - Spend as much face-time with as many people as you can
   - Bond with your immediate teammates, but also spiral outward
2. **Deliver a quick win**

   The size of the deed is not important. What is: Building a reputation as someone who delivers above and beyond – with as little supervision as possible
3. **Under promise, over deliver**
4. **Set a personal 100-day goal, separate from whatever your manager expects**

   Can be big or small, but have a personal goal. Make your mark
5. **Celebrate other people's successes**

   Your time for notoriety will come. Shine a light on your teammates' wins

4

During your First Day meeting with your manager, ask for a Two-Way Review at the end of your third month

Ideally, this should be a part of your formal performance reviews. If that's not possible, play it low key. Have an informal conversation. But make sure it happens! Your goal is to partner with your manager to ensure you both learn from this experience and can plan the next few months. (That's why it's two-way: The review isn't just about *your* performance. You also want the opportunity to talk with your manager about how s/he can better help you succeed.)

WHAT'S BEHIND DOING LESS

Jamie has a confession that will embarrass her bosses (so that's not her real name). She works for a globally recognized company that's on several *100 Best Companies to Work For* lists. She's helped design and roll out a terrific orientation program that mirrors everything in this chapter. "The principles in our program revolve around helping every new hire have the courage to lead their manager in the kinds of conversations they need to have," she reports.

"There's a huge emphasis on helping people build the networks and relationships they need sooner rather than later. We ask their managers to have an interview plan prepared for them. [See 20 Names, Step 3.] We also try to provide them with the space and time to help them understand what they'll need to know and how they'll be supported. We also follow them through their first few months, and survey them about their experiences." Jamie's senior leadership team not only supports this program, they cite it as one of the ways they'll earn future *Best Company* accolades.

Sounds great! So what could Jamie possibly have to confess? "Most of our leaders and managers still don't see any value in this program. They see it as a win/lose situation. By giving their new hires the space and time to 'gaze into their navels' (as one manager described it to me), that means they don't get enough of the new hires' time. They're so short-staffed as it is, they simply can not afford to free up their valuable new resources."

•

Ah...There's the rub!

Every company and every leader understands, intellectually, that it's in their *long-term* interest to create this type of orientation. (Higher morale, better retention, faster learning, etc.) Yet not many are willing to sacrifice their short-term needs (fasterfaster, moremoremore) for long-term returns.

And even fewer are willing to drive longer-term thinking throughout their culture. (SAS and Jet Blue Airlines are current stellar exceptions.) And even great cultures, that do "get it," can quickly fall apart. Since its founding in 1978, The Home Depot was heralded for

THE WAY OUT:  **EXECUTIVE COUNTER-MOVES**

If you're a senior executive, and want to change the way orientation gets done in your company, here's how to use the advice in this chapter:

1. **Hold your managers accountable for the success of every new hire's orientation**
   Not just the first day: the first 100 days.
2. **Provide templates for 20 good names**
   Managers may need guidance as to what types of people should be on a networking list.
3. **Provide templates for homework assignments**
   Define the types of information that can be shared in the new hire's homework. (Note: If these templates are too sanitized, you'll defeat the purpose. New hires should get the good and the bad and the ugly. The full truth, warts and all.)

its employee- and customer-focused culture. Until CEO Bob Nardelli arrived from General Electric in 2000 and GEized everything. Currently (depending on who you ask), employee morale and customer satisfaction have fallen anywhere between 10% to 40%.

•

Don't wait for the company to "get it."

More than likely: You're on your own

I'd like nothing better than to fill this chapter with heart-warming Jet Blue–type orientation stories and promise you that there are lots of companies out there that know how to do new hire orientations. But I'd be creating false hope.

The odds are that you will have a different experience, and that you are going to have to redesign whatever is thrown at you. Even well-intentioned companies like Jamie's have a hard time pushing past the short-term pressures, ensuring the success of your orientation. That's why the steps in this chapter are so important:

- **Doing homework before your first day**
- **Getting a list of 20 names**
- **Asking for a three-month check in**

If you want greater satisfaction out of your work, and you want to be better at your job, assume these three things as your responsibility. Treat whatever else the company puts into orientation as a bonus.

WANT MORE?

Worthwhile Sidetrips

Redesigning your orientation is about improving the connections between your wants and needs, your work, you and your teammates, you and your company. To fully explore those connections, some sidetrips may be in order:

- *The Four Obsessions of an Extraordinary Executive,* by Patrick Lencioni
- *A Company of Citizens,* by Brook Manville, Josiah Ober
- *The Purpose-Driven Life: What on Earth Am I Here For?,* by Rick Warren

16

How to
Clarify Your Goals and Objectives More Quickly

LESS•O•METERS

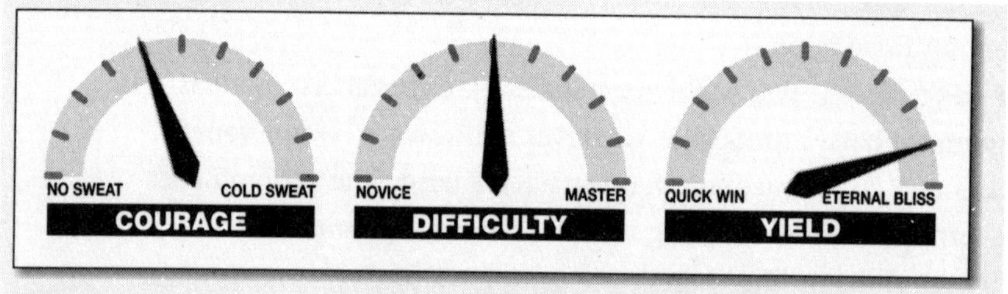

STEPS: 5

TAKEAWAY: Ask the 5 questions that will get you the clarity you need

KEEPING SCORE: Do not take on work until you get clarity

WHY DO LESS

You already know that fuzzy and foggy goals are a pain in the butt, and a huge source of work complexity[1] • But do you know how to stop taking on work until you create clarity?

Pre-Work

It's usually not the goals themselves that are unclear.

What you're supposed to do with them is what's fuzzy — how the goals refocus or change your work.

To figure that out, you need to ask the five questions of Behavioral Communication…

Bottom line: Do not take on work until you understand what the goals mean to you, and the kind of work you should be doing.

That doesn't mean refusing work. It means pushing for clarity.

HOW TO DO LESS

❶

As soon as your boss sets a new goal for you, or tells you about a new corporate objective, ask:

Help me understand how this changes what I've been doing?

Most managers can only clarify goals from the *company's* or *department's* perspective. You need to understand the relevance of this new goal — exactly how *your* job, *your* duties, *your* focus, *your* energies, and *your* use of time need to change.

For example: If you're a call-center manager, and the boss is rah-rah'ing your team about innovation goals, ask "How does the company's new focus on innovation change how I manage handle-time on customer calls?" If a company goal is relevant to your work, you have to understand how it affects how you do your job, and if you will be expected to change your focus.

❶ a

If the answer you get still isn't clear to you, take the answer and ask "Why?" up to five times

(See Chapter 11 for more about Why?)

2

Then ask:

Got suggestions for my first steps?

What's the best way to get started?

This isn't about you waiting to be handed a checklist of mandated activities. You've got a head on your shoulders and you should be using it. Instead, this question is about probing for immediate next steps. "There are fourteen things that need to get done, which ones should I do first?" or "Could you help me break this goal down to what I should do this week?" You are like most everyone in this overworked, overloaded environment: You can figure out a lot on your own, but some guidance on where to focus your energies first will help jumpstart your efforts. So ask for your immediate next steps.

2 a

If you're still not clear on what you should do, ask "Why?" up to five times

3

Then ask:

What does success look like?...What should I watch for to be sure I'm making progress, and am on target?

This question helps you understand how organizational success relates to *you*: "OK, we need to improve customer satisfaction by 10%. Could you help me understand what that looks like for me? How will I know that I'm being successful in moving us closer to that goal? Will you come tell me? Will I hear something different from customers? And how will I know if I screw up? I certainly want to prevent that! Can you tell me what to watch out for?" You need to know what *your* success looks like — not just the overall corporate measure of success — before you take on a job.

An easy way to get beyond management-speak is to use two of your five senses. Ask your manager "What will I *see* that will indicate to me that I'm heading towards success" and "What will I *hear*?" That will move the definition of success beyond corporate-run metrics, and into something that you can observe all by yourself.

3 a

If that's still not clear to you, repeatedly ask "Why?"

Behavioral Communication

THE MOST-ASKED QUESTION ABOUT THE FIVE QUESTIONS

Which one is most important to most people?

You thought it was WIIFM, didn't you? C'mon, admit it. That's what many believe. Wrong-o.

The most-asked question is the least-answered question: Tools and support.

The biggest struggle people have is not how corporate goals will also enrich them, but how they're going to get everything done. So if you're a manager, and you're trying to help others, and you only have time to answer one question — make it tools and support. From there, everyone can figure out more of their own answers.

- How is this relevant to what I do?
- What, specifically, should I do?
- What do success and failure look like?
- What tools and support are available?
- WIIFM — What's in it for me?

4

Then ask:

What tools and support are available?

This is all about execution — getting everything done. You may be thinking: "I'm working 29 hours a day, 10 days a week, and you just put something *more* on my plate?!?! How the hell am I supposed to get all this done?"

While you may want to react that way, I wouldn't advise it. A more constructive approach (that will get you what you're after) is to focus on whatever enablers, tools, and support your company has in place to help you. A partial list:

- Project kick-off meeting
- Brainstorming session
- Training
- IT (Intranet, web-based tools, etc.)
- One-on-one meetings with manager
- Mentoring
- Communities of practice
- Information templates
- Project sponsors
- Temporary teammates
- Dedicated space/place
- Research data

Frankly, you will never have enough tools and support. That's reality, baby. But you must discover *whatever is available* before starting your work. Getting the right tools, at the right time, in the right way will help you get everything done.

4 a

Change-up:

Do NOT ask "Why?" when you discover how few tools and support are available, or if you discover there's no WIIFM. (See below)

The only possible answers will reflect poorly on your manager, or your company, or both. And prolonging the conversation will just frustrate you.

5

Final question:

WIIFM — What's in it for me? Or for us?

I'm sure you know to phrase this question properly. Some approaches include, "Help me understand how this helps me achieve my goals?" and "How does this help our team be more successful?" Push for clarity here. All human beings are motivated, in part, by self-interest — the need for rewards, inclusion, or recognition. I've found that the reward most people crave is not money, but personal fulfillment: Less stress. More fun. Making more of a difference. Higher personal standards on workmanship. More time with one's family, etc. Whichever is your prime motivator, push to discover how your new project will deliver it.

Reality check: We all do some work that we *have* to do — chores that don't meet our personal needs, and aren't very rewarding. That's life. So asking the WIIFM question doesn't mean that every project must be satisfying. However, it does help you identify *patterns*. Are five out of every ten projects satisfying your long-term needs? Not bad! Are nine out of every ten just drudgery? Then maybe you should think about getting a new job. Asking WIIFM? helps you keep track of your own fulfillment every time you take on an assignment.

THE WAY OUT:  **EXECUTIVE COUNTER-MOVES**

If you're a senior executive, and want all employees to understand their goals, **go to the Do-Less Toolkit, tear out the Behavioral Communication model, and make sure you help your managers answer those five questions.** Because the answers are the difference between truly clear goals and "Uh huh. Sure, I can parrot back what my goals are. But I have no idea what they really mean!"

WHAT'S BEHIND DOING LESS

"During my first two years here, I had to figure out what my goals were. They weren't very clear, and asking my manager didn't help. She didn't know either," says Thomas, who works for the same *Best Company to Work For* as Jamie, whom we met in Chapter 15.

Manager: *You need to prepare a list of your goals for this year.*

Thomas: *Well, I really want to work on things that'll help the department succeed. What are your goals for this year?*

Manager: *I haven't done mine yet. But I can give you a copy of last year's goals.*

Thomas: *(To himself) Not only did she not get it, she didn't even realize there was an it to get!*

Thomas's boss is the division's General Manager, so he has daily access to the company's strategic plans. And yet: "I couldn't figure out what to do with the strategic plan," says Thomas. "I got more and more frustrated, feeling like a worker bee — jumping on any directive that came down to me because I wasn't getting clear direction from my manager."

Thomas's plight is fairly common. During our study, we found that the Number Two source of work complexity was unclear goals and objectives. As his job so perfectly illustrates, clarity doesn't mean access to or explanations of the strategic plan. Clarity means: *Translate this for me. What do these goals mean to me, and what am I supposed to do with them?*

This is where most people are actually complicit in their own work complexity. We found that most employees wait for someone to do the translating for them. Employees who are proactive, who jump in and ask enough questions to create their own clarity eliminate this source of complexity. Lesson learned: Jump in. Don't wait for translations.

Thomas learned this lesson: "One day, I just had enough. I started asking questions that were really statements in disguise…'This part of the strategic plan is relevant to what you want me to do, right?…These are the resources I've got available, right?'…I bulleted what I felt I needed to be clear about, and asked for her concurrence. She changed a few things, and disagreed with me on one point. But that was alright. At least I knew what she wanted, and that gave me focus. I started to feel like I was more in control, and less like I was being dumped on."

•

The power of five questions

As much as you'd like your manager to be a great translator — clarifying what a company-wide goal means just to you — s/he is just as crazed, overloaded, and crunched as you are. Maybe more. The power of the five questions of Behavioral Communication is that you become the translator. You may find that this also changes your relationship with your boss. Thomas concludes, "Now, my manager has a lot more confidence in me. She knows I've moved from being task-driven, to helping her look good."

•

The only caveat

Clarity doesn't guarantee happiness. You may find that you don't like or agree with the answers you get. As long as this only happens occasionally, shrug it off and move on. But if you find a pattern of unhappiness and disagreement, that's where the rest of this book kicks in. Maybe you should be saying no more often, or voting with your feet. The only guarantee you get with clarity is that you're accountable for acting upon whatever you've learned.

WANT MORE?

Tear out the Behavioral Communication page in the Do-Less Toolkit. Tack it up in your cube. Refer to it anytime you take on new projects.

17

How to

Deal with Managers Who Pile It On: MoreMoreMore, Now!

LESS•O•METERS

STEPS: 4

TAKEAWAY: You can reduce the flow of work from your manager

KEEPING SCORE: You can do more of what you'll be evaluated on, and ignore the rest

WHY DO LESS

Managers who fail to prioritize and focus your workload **are abdicating a responsibility** they have to you • Still, partnering with your manager will reduce your workload • Complaining will not

HOW TO DO LESS

1

Before you talk with your boss about managing your workload:
Do your homework

Know *exactly* which work is extraneous, how many goals are too many, and where you think your efforts need to be focused.

Some guidelines for doing your homework, and figuring out what's extraneous and what's important:

- **Nobody can focus on more than three to five goals at a time**
  Of the umpteen goals your manager just announced, which three do you believe will add the most value to the company, your customers, your team, and you?
- **All work requires tools, support, training, and resources**
  Itemize your entire workload. Which projects are so under-supported that they are doomed to fail? Which projects lack true sponsorship and commitment from key players in the organization? By answering those two questions, you've identified your extraneous workload.
- **Research tip:** Ask for copies of whatever communication, reports, presentations your manager presents to his bosses. Even if he hasn't focused your to-do's to a critical few, the odds are that *his* few priorities are in those reports! And his few need to be your few.

2

When you meet with your manager,
acknowledge the pressures s/he must be under

A spoonful of sugar helps the medicine go down.
Be empathetic to how important all the goals must be, and how all the work must get done at some point.

3

Ask:

"Can we talk about which three things should be my top focus for the next few [days, weeks or months]?"

You can succeed! The secret...

- Pick a short timeframe, and
- Do not ask your manager to rethink goals or workload that have been handed down to him

Something like...

Hey boss, I know we're supposed to get these 4,321 things done within the next few months, and I'd never question the wisdom of this list (...ahem...), but I've got some suggestions for which three should be my priority for the next few weeks. Of course, (...ahem...), I'll keep the other 4,318 moving forward while I focus on these three.

(For more on "ahem," see Smile and Nod strategy in Chapter 12)

Or...

These are the three things I'd recommend we focus on first. Make sense?

(Of course, your Pass-On-Too-Much manager will want to up your three things to five or ten or twenty. On to Step 4...)

4

Keep shortening the timeframe (from months to weeks to, possibly, days) until, as partners, you both agree: "These three."

Don't challenge the length of the entire list or your manager's inability to prioritize. Instead, just keep narrowing the timeframe...

Boss, thanks for helping me see that there's only 347 things that have to get done this month. Now, can we talk about which to-do's need to be checked off by this Friday? ...Only 47? Great! Now, which three of those should I focus on first?

continued on page 146

Laws•O•Less

Once begun, work follows the path of least resistance.

Most of us manage our daily workload through triage:
We avoid or postpone all but the most pressing decisions and tasks. And when everybody is in triage mode, **the path of least resistance is to just keep things moving,** passing work on to others as quickly as possible, even if that work comes up short in focus or importance. Because the **biggest wall of resistance** comes from stopping the flow and telling our bosses what they want us to do isn't focused, important, or valid.

The So What? Law of Doing Less

It's a lot easier than you think to reduce the flow of work from your boss.

The secret is to *avoid* any conversations that sound like you want to reduce the flow of work from his plate onto yours, and instead just *clarify* the immediate next steps. Clarification is your secret partnering tool — while your boss is clarifying next steps, he'll actually get more focused. Really!

The Search for a Simpler Way: Between 1998 and 2003, we asked over 750 people to rank order the ten most common workplace behaviors we had observed since 1992.
After they ranked *Moving To-Do's Onto Someone Else's Plate,* we asked "How come?....Why do people do that?" The Third Law of Workplace Behavior emerged from their responses.

4 *continued*

Or…

Based on our long-term objective, I think these three things need to be done first, as a foundation for everything else. Make sense?

Most people avoid dealing with their manager's inability to get focused because they don't know how to confront the problem without confronting the person. By continually narrowing the timeframe, you can get your manager to prioritize *without* going toe-to-toe. It's an indirect approach that some have called the Nibble Method: taking small steps to get priorities set.

The upside is that you avoid confrontation. The downside: you'll have to continually go back for another nibble of focus. That's why some prefer a more direct method…

Hey boss, I'm not leaving your office until you cut this whole list down to just three things.

(See Leadership Lessons sidebar for this approach)

…If that works for you, go for it! Both approaches yield the same thing — less work, greater focus. The only difference is where you spend your energy.

People who have followed the steps in this chapter report a success rate of 80%, and better, in dealing with managers who pass on too much [1]

Instead of saying "no" to too much work, these people have figured out that if they partner with their manager on setting better priorities, they actually reduce the overall flow of work that comes at them.

Equally important, they find that the vital few priorities they coaxed out of their manager end up being the ones on which they're evaluated at year's end.

WHAT'S BEHIND DOING LESS

The key to success is **knowing what NOT to do.** The steps in this chapter have been specifically designed to stop you from shooting yourself in the foot!

If you work with a manager who continually passes on too much, don't question your workload, or push for anything greater than short-term prioritization! If you do, **your manager is likely to think that you're pushing work *back* onto his or her plate!** Then, *everything* that happens next — the negotiations, the kicking and screaming, all the business rationale, everything — has *absolutely nothing* to do with your goals or your workload. Instead, what's buzzing through your manager's head is "Geez, I thought I got this off my plate and onto yours! Are you asking me to revisit decisions that I've already made? I don't have time for that!"

It's *his* workload he's worried about, not yours!

That's the Third Law of Workplace behavior in action: Once begun, work follows the path of least resistance — your boss is in triage mode, and doesn't want anything pushed back on his plate. He wants you to just keep things moving.

To further demonstrate the Third Law in action, let's take you out of the picture. Here's a conversation your manager has with himself every day…

Let's see, I have a gazillion things to do today, including this brainstorming meeting for Project Alpha. Do I really want to spend time examining whether my boss was clear when turning Project Alpha over to me, or whether this initiative will solve the real problem that our customers want us to address, or whether I need to refocus and

reshape Alpha's goals to be more realistic to the time and resources that are available to me?

Nahhhhhh.

I don't wanna go there. Those kind of questions mean I'd probably have to go back to my boss, and maybe his boss. And for what — more headaches? No, let's just have our meeting, and keep things moving full-speed ahead.

Now, imagine you could see the thought bubbles above *everyone's* heads — including yours and your teammates'. You'd see the exact same conversation!

One of the primary drivers in day-to-day activities is to keep things moving forward. Most of us avoid anything that smacks of *moving backwards* — like stopping to reflect on, and question, any work that has already been set in motion.

That doesn't make any of us bad people. Or bad managers or bad teammates. Just crazed and overloaded.

•

How not to shoot yourself in the foot

Unless you are willing to go toe-to-toe with your manager — forcing him to think about his own workload — avoid conversations that ask your manager to uncheck his handoff to you. You don't want to appear to be pushing anything back onto his plate. The four steps in this chapter will help you avoid this. (Note: In some "empowered" cultures, you may be able to push back on your manager. If you're among the lucky few — great! Do so. But it's an extremely rare manager who is willing to have his decisions questioned, *especially* if it means pushing work back onto his boss's plate.)

•

Overload creates opportunities

Accept the fact that too much work is probably going to keep coming at you. But because your manager hasn't had the time to think through your entire workload, that leaves a window of opportunity to jump in and **clarify upcoming, short-term To-Do's.** If you keep the timeframe short enough, most every manager appreciates help in clarifying what comes next. For example…

"My job is about results. Most of my team, no matter how much coaching I provide, just tackles whatever tasks I give them. But the new guy, Jamaal, he's great! He checks in with me regularly with a one-page checklist he made himself. At the top are our plant goals. Then on the left, he's got a running list of this quarter's biggest priorities, and on the right, what he thinks should be his top priorities for the next few weeks. We don't always agree. But I really appreciate how he comes in prepared, and how much time he saves me."

– Manufacturing plant foreman

•

Do your homework. Tackle short-term, bite-size chunks of prioritization. And make it easy for your manager to approve your suggestions. Save him time and don't make him think he's got to go to his boss, and you will be able to continually redirect the flow of work coming at you. I promise! (A promise that I can guarantee because of the First Law of Workplace Behavior: Make it easier for people to do things your way, and you'll get your way more often.)

WANT MORE?

Basic Tips

- If you still hear "Everything's a priority — do all of it," reread Chapters 5 and 10. You will find that the five questions of Behavioral Communication and the Indirect Approach to saying "no" are invaluable tools.

When Sucking Up Matters

- *Managing Up,* by Rosanne Badowski
  An insider's views on kissing up, sucking up, and self-management. Badowski was GE CEO Jack Welch's long-time executive assistant

Leadership Lessons in Doing Less

Janiece Webb
Senior Vice President, Personal Networks Group
Motorola

Respect Yourself: Keep Pushing for the Vital Few

"So many people confuse activity with results. Yet, if you stop doing everything but the most essential work, it's actually career-enhancing. People really respect people who work smart, not hard. If you are consumed with bureaucratic BS, you can't have an impact because you don't have the time.

"Working smarter means saying, 'I can't do everything.' Constantly finding the vital few, and focusing on those.

"I just came out from under a boss who gave me forty MBO targets [Management by Objective], and I refused to accept that. We wrestled for six months. During several tough meetings, I said to him that I would only do three of the targets. (Knowing that I'd accept five.) I told him all the rest were nice-to-do's, not the vital few.

"In our first meeting, he said that everything was important. I acknowledged, without any disparaging comments, that all the targets were important. But I said I just can't do all of them. And that my poor execution would put him at risk. I asked if others could take on some of the targets. Eventually, he agreed to reduce the list by about 25 percent. But that still left too many MBOs. Even though I thought a lot of the list was dumb, I said 'Let me go back and see what's possible.'

"I looked into what it would take to do the remaining targets. I began our second meeting by telling him that most everything on the list was a lot harder than we might have realized, and I walked him through a few examples. Again, I said that I just couldn't get all this done. Again, I asked 'Who else can we assign this to?' I kept forcing him to choose. 'Which one of these do you think is most important? Which one of these…?' One by one, I crossed things off. He let me get away with reducing the list to a reasonable number, but he didn't really mean it. After our meeting, I learned from my team that he was still communicating all the targets I got him to take off the list.

"So during our third meeting, I was relentless. 'What do you want me to take off my plate? Which ones do you want me to kill? Do we have an agreement that we're only going to focus on these five?' Then, I went behind the scenes to check with other executives that we had, indeed, selected the vital few. That way, when we had operations reviews with his boss, the only thing we'd talk about were those top five.

"Not long after, this guy was removed from his job! And the first thing my new boss said was 'We're not going to confuse activity with results. We will have impact. You will have only three to five goals, but they are going to be big ones. And hard ones. And I don't care about the nice-to-do's. We're going to focus.'

"This is a classic example of why it's so important to push until you get to the vital few. My previous boss was always too busy, in at 7am and didn't leave until 8 or 9pm. Our new leader has a more balanced family life and is much more respected.

"In the end, your bosses get rewarded for work that really matters. If you push to the vital few, you're making them look good. And for me, life is too precious to let a job drag me and my family down. You've got to like yourself. You've got to respect yourself. You've got to walk your own talk."

18

How to

Deal with Teammates Who (Unknowingly) Pile It On

LESS•O•METERS

STEPS: 4

TAKEAWAY: Push back by clarifying

KEEPING SCORE: Score 30% to 50% reduction in to-do's from teammates

WHY DO LESS

Your best friends and trusted teammates don't mean to add to your to-do's • Really!

But right after unfocused managers, your biggest source of overload are those well-intentioned teammates

Pre-Work

Always assume that your teammates have taken the path of least resistance. Eight times out of ten, you'll be right.[1]

Recapping the highlights from Chapter 17, which will be applied here:

- Once begun, work follows the path of least resistance. This means that many of your teammates are focused on whatever gets work off their plate the fastest. And, if what they've been asked to do lacks clarity, focus, or importance, they know they'll encounter less resistance by keeping things moving forward — onto your plate — than if they went back to their boss and questioned what they've been handed.
- Following the path of least resistance doesn't make anyone a bad person, a bad manager, or a bad teammate. Just someone who's crazed, overloaded, and coping as best they can.

HOW TO DO LESS

1

Trust your gut for the first cut.

Not your head

When they first meet with you, your teammates will repeat the corporate mantras of cost-cutting and strategic focus and blah, blah, blah. OK, fine. Let your head buy into all that so you can be a good corporate citizen. But if you feel a tightness in your stomach, and you have to suppress thoughts like "Gee, I've got too much to do already," then trust your gut.

•

Use your gut. Cover your butt.

The queasiness is sending you a message: although your teammates may be well-intentioned, they may have taken the path of least resistance — and not thought through the things that will bite you in the butt down the road. Like passing along unrealistic expectations, or being unclear themselves about priorities, measures, or political landmines associated with the work.

•

Spring into Clarify Mode.

Your best shot for redirecting the flow of work coming at you is to start helping your teammates clarify and focus the to-do's that lie ahead.

❷

Seek clarity on the team's upcoming to-do's.

Focus on the short-term — the next few days' or next few weeks' to-do's. Focus on two areas:

- Clarify how the team's to-do's relate back to overall success
- Clarify how the team's to-do's help pass this project onto someone else

  (There is *always* someone else. Your teammates may be handing off to other internal teams, or to other employees, or to customers, or back up the chain of command, or outside partners, or, or, or…)

How? You are already familiar with the tools you need from previous chapters…

CHAPTERS	CLARIFY	HOW TO CLARIFY
5 11	**How the next steps assigned to you and others relate to overall success**	• Asking the five questions of Behavioral Communication • Asking Why? up to five times to expose the full truth
3 5	**How the next steps will help pass this project on to others**	• Helping to clarify what others will Know, Feel, Do • Helping your teammates be CLEAR

I guarantee that, if you ask the questions laid out in those chapters, you will find holes in your To-Do's big enough to drive a truck through! Holes like:

- Unclear connections to your own goals and what you'll be measured on
- Unclear next steps
- Unclear definition of success for the project
- Lack of clarity and focus on which tools and support would be most helpful
- Lack of clarity around how this project's outcomes will be handed off to others

❸

Shhhhhh.

Don't tell anyone that you're deflecting and deferring.

You're about to be applauded for how you helped everyone get focused

- *Ya know…Instead of doing these seven things, I think we'd get more bang for our buck if we focused on these two. That's what our senior team is focused on, right?*
- *It sounds like we're trying to accomplish too much here. Shouldn't our short-term definition of success be tighter?*
- *All this is great. But guys, our main deliverable is to Alpha Team. We're focused on apples and Alpha Team needs oranges. I think, ultimately, we'd be more successful if we narrowed our scope to meet their needs.*

You are practicing enlightened self-interest. Because your teammates are so overloaded, they are coming to you with too many to-do's. Yet that same overload creates an opportunity. If you help your colleagues create bite-sized chunks of short-term clarity, they will salute you! By focusing and reducing your own work, you are helping everyone move things off their plate more quickly because they're more focused. Win, win. (Remember: Shhhhhhhh….)

People who follow these three steps with their teammates report a 30% to 50% reduction in to-do's from those teammates[2]

4

Rejoice!

Celebrate!

You just achieved a major career milestone

Following these steps can be a boon to your career. The moment to watch for is when you fine-tune your ability to **push back on requests and ideas from close teammates *in such a way* that they ask for more pushback!**

If there was ever a guaranteed job-for-life, it is reserved for those who clarify quickly and get people focused more quickly. Master the steps in this chapter and you will be amazed by the demand for your services!

WHAT'S BEHIND DOING LESS

As we have seen in previous chapters…(heck, as you know from real life!)…**hardly anyone is as focused as they need to be.** And, if you're not vigilant, all the problems that your teammates missed in their rush to keep things moving will end up on your plate.

This happens with even the best of teammates in the best of cultures. As long as they, like you, are competing in an environment of morebetterfaster, no one is immune.

So there's a demand for people at all levels of the organization who can walk into a meeting or dial into a teleconference, quickly assess what's unfocused, and jump in with suggestions to help everyone reduce their priorities to the vital few.

Lee-Ang's story is a perfect example. She works for a globally recognized technology firm and was asked to join a team charged with changing the company's performance management measures. The change meant that it would be tougher to achieve an "Exceeds Expectations" ranking. And the team asked Lee-Ang to help figure out how this could be communicated to managers and employees in such a way that they would feel confident and comfortable with these new standards.

During a three-hour meeting, she sat silently. Her team members had been describing the new performance plan, and they were quite proud of how they had reduced all the details down to just forty pages, and ten key messages that the managers would then communicate to their troops. After she heard everything she said, "I have three questions. First, is there any one thing that would make this program succeed or fail?" The team stumbled through some guesses, and eventually narrowed it down to "The conversation that the manager has with the employee. That's the key." She then asked her second question, "What needs to be different about that conversation?" This time, without hesitation, one of her teammates answered, "Managers need to talk with their employees at much deeper levels about their performance. And we're helping them do that."

Lee-Ang asked her final question while dropping hundreds of PowerPoint pages onto the floor. "Then why are we spending so much time trying to get the managers to understand all this plan minutia that only you care about? Why aren't we organizing everything around what they really need to know: 'How to Change the Conversation'?"

Everyone in the room suddenly realized that Lee-Ang had just reduced their workload, refocused everyone's energy, and made everything easier to hand off to managers and employees. They still had to address the details that were in all those PowerPoint slides, but they were now able to look at those details from the *manager's perspective, not their own*. That change greatly sped up how quickly they were able to get this project off their plates.

Lee-Ang's story is not unique. Everywhere, teammates talking to teammates need help in getting focused, and reducing their workload to only what's critical. Everywhere, the solution isn't within the strategic objectives or something that's handed down from above. It will come from the one teammate who asks the right questions, probes for clarity, and helps everyone see what's really important.

Will that teammate be you?

WANT MORE?

Basic Tips

- Reread Chapters 3, 5, and 11.

  You'll find the tools you need to help you help your teammates.

19

How to
Track Your Success: Are You Really Doing Less?

LESS•O•METERS

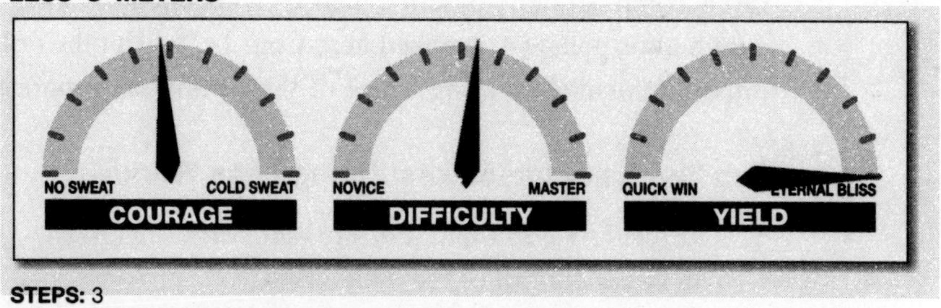

STEPS: 3

TAKEAWAY: Know *why* you're doing less

KEEPING SCORE: Define success for *yourself*, not your to-do's

TIME FOR A PROGRESS CHECK

How will you know you're doing less and accomplishing more? • It's an important question! • Most people spend too little time thinking about what success looks like

HOW TO TRACK SUCCESS

1

Let's say you've tried a few of the workarounds in this book. And you're feeling good… real good! Do you know why? In Step 2, you'll figure it out. But not yet. For now, just…

Heighten your senses.

Listen to conversations differently.

Watch behaviors — yours and others'.

How many of the Top Ten Early Indicators do you recognize?

The following are how people who have taken steps to do less so they can accomplish more describe their own experiences. The most common responses are ranked here from 1–10.[1] But the order is less important than identifying which of these represent progress *for you.*

Top Ten Early Indicators: Doing Less Works!

1. "I feel less burnt out, less stressed. More energized. In better control of the daily grind."
   Representative quote from Maria, a senior vice president in an insurance company

2. "I'm making better choices, setting better priorities."
   Representative quote from Tom, a blue-collar employee in a steel mill

3. "I believe in myself more. I better understand what I can and can't do."
   Representative quote from Marc, a financial manager in an automobile firm

4. "I've gotten others to respect my valuable time."
   Representative quote from Quan, a mid-manager at a financial services firm

5. "I finally feel I can be authentic in what I do and say. I've stopped playing the game."
   Representative quote from Franz, a senior manager in a pharmaceuticals company

6. "I finally know what's propaganda, what's BS, and what's a flavor of the month. That's so liberating!"
Representative quote from Dave, a foreman in a printing plant

7. "I can now set expectations with my boss as well as with my teammates."
Representative quote from Renaldo, a mid-manager for a hotel conglomerate

8. "Those I manage tell me I'm more focused, and that they enjoy their work more."
Representative quote from Pilar, a mid-manager in a software firm

9. "I feel I can say 'No' more often, and stick to it."
Representative quote from Dumas, a front-line employee in a telecommunications firm

10. "I'm helping others more than I used to."
Representative quote from Keiko, a mid-manager in a textiles firm

Do any of these quotes describe what you've experienced? If so, you've made great progress! These are early indicators that you're on the right track. You're ready for Step 2....

2

Now ask yourself, "So what?"
It's time to decide what to do with all that good feeling. Use it to think deeply about how you define success, and what it truly means to you

During our interviews, we found two conflicting themes in the ways people evaluate their success in doing less. The majority, more than six in ten,[2] define success with a checklist — to-do's done more quickly, or not at all, or passed on to others. Most of your coworkers just want the stress and overload to go away. They're not looking beyond their checklist.

People who take this approach feel like they *never truly succeed*. "There's always more to do," says Michael, a retail executive. "As soon as I get work off my plate, twice as much gets loaded back on.

I feel like I'm only able to do less occasionally, on certain days, with certain work. My bosses, customers, and endless cost-cutting always force me to take on more." People like Michael are never able to *sustain* their quick wins in doing less.

However, almost four out of every ten of your teammates take a different approach, and *are* able to sustain their successes. While they do need to get stuff off their plate, and check off to-do's, that's not how they view success. They begin with an end in mind. They have a goal, and all that matters is progress toward the goal. And that goal is almost always personal, never corporate.

While there are as many personal definitions of success as there are people, during our interviews we found three that were most common:

•

"Work is important, but it is not life.
I want the time and ability to focus on my family, friends, community, and all that life can offer."

Unlike the popular term, *work/life balance*, not everyone is interested in an equal balance between work and life. For many people, work is just a means to an end. Examples of this goal range from a single mom whose sole focus is providing for the future of her daughters, to a twenty-something tech-worker who lives to travel, to Dave, a printing plant foreman who loves rebuilding cars on Saturdays and donating his time to church projects on Sundays.

Is your goal to do less at work so you can do more outside of work?

•

"I want to make a difference.
I need to know that whatever I do matters, and is truly important."

Most of us want to be part of something bigger than ourselves. We want our contributions to matter, and we want to take pride in whatever we do. Unfortunately, many people are growing disillusioned or frustrated with what employers believe is important. Says Keiko, a mid-manager in a textiles plant, "That's why I'm ignoring so much from all these ad-hoc teams. They want me to cut more costs. For what? So we save a few bucks this month and destroy people in the process? I'm here to help people. I can do that more effectively by spending more time coaching and mentoring the people who work for me. If I do that well, I'll save the company more money in the long run."

Is your goal to do less of what you know, in your heart, is merely urgent and not important — so you can do more of what you know actually matters?

•

"I want to be the best that I can be. What excites me is always learning, improving, and challenging myself."

The most creative and/or driven people seem to have the lowest tolerance for non-value-added work. Says Quan, a mid-manager in a financial services firm, "I can do what I do for anybody on The Street. The reason I've stayed for years at this firm, but only lasted months at others, is the opportunity I have for growth. I'm the kind of person who needs a challenge. So far, I'm getting that here. If that ever changes, I'll bail no matter how much I'm paid."

Is your goal to do less non-value-added work, so you feel more fulfilled, exhilarated, challenged, and alive?

•

Or is your goal something else entirely? The goal you choose isn't the point. The point is that you choose one. If you want success to last longer than the time it takes to read this paragraph, stop tracking what's on or off your plate. Have a goal. Begin with the end in mind, and track your progress toward it.

3

Need another step to nail down that goal?

Take the three basic reasons for doing less...

- Work is important, but it is not life. I want to focus on all life has to offer.
- I want to make a difference. The work I do must matter.
- I want to be the best I can be.

...to your family, mentor, coach, or closest friend.

Ask them which best describes you.

Whatever they answer, ask them "Why?" at least three times.

They will help you discover your own passion and reasons for doing less. Those reasons will help you focus your efforts and sustain your successes.

I have had long conversations with mentors and coaches. Each and every one has said the same thing: unless you know what you want, and are happy with yourself, you will be stuck doing stuff in non-productive ways (that you wish you could get out of). When you put this book down, please don't think about checklists or emails or meetings or other daily nonsense. Think about how you define success and why you do what you do. Please.

WHAT'S BEHIND DOING LESS

Some of you will probably think I'm bonkers for having buried this chapter in the middle of the book. Obviously — if we want people to begin with the end in mind — a chapter on setting goals and figuring out why it's important to do less should be at the front of the book, right?

Bonkers or not, the placement was intentional.

After years of observing interviews, workshops, meetings, and work, I've found that most of us (at least six out of ten) are more willing to do self-reflection *after* we've experienced some quick successes. I wanted that majority (you know who you are!) to experience a few quick wins in deleting emails or saying no before pushing this self-reflection to the foreground.

Quick, easy wins are important — a good lesson to remember since, at some point, you too will ask others to look in the mirror. It'll be a lot easier to get people to self-reflect, if you first help them successfully get stuff off their plate. Then they'll feel they have the time to kick back and reflect.

WANT  **MORE?**

Power Tips

A few of many sources for deeper self-reflection:

- *The Places That Scare You,* by Pema Chodron
- *Man's Search for Meaning,* by Viktor Frankl
- *The Power of Now,* by Eckhart Tolle
- *The CEO and the Monk,* by Kenny Moore (see Leadership Lesson)

Leadership Lessons in Doing Less

Kenny Moore

Corporate Ombudsman, HR Director

KeySpan

- Former monk
- Survived "incurable" cancer as well as open-heart surgery
- Having dealt with both God and death, he finds himself eminently qualified to work with executives on corporate change efforts

Only the Important Things Really Matter

"For more than thirty years, my career has been involved with life's deep questions: What is our vocation? How do we make a living and not lose our soul in the process? Can our businesses make the world a better place for our children? What will be our legacy after we're gone? I help others answer these questions for themselves.

"In 1982, after spending 15 years in a monastic community as a Catholic priest, I found that I, too, was facing these questions. I was unhappy in the priesthood. I was going through the motions, but had lost my way. I remember saying mass to the community one day, looking out, and saying to myself, 'I don't think I believe the same things these people do.' The feeling I had was like I was on a boxcar headed for Dachau. And the people who put me there were those in authority, saying 'No, it's just a relocation camp, and your luggage will soon be following you.' And I got on this train thinking 'If I stay here I'm going to die.' So the question was, should I jump or stay? The problem with jumping from the priesthood is that, unlike from a company, the people you leave behind truly are family. It was a difficult decision, but ultimately I decided it was time to go.

"Eventually, I ended up at a gas and electric company. I was hired to design and implement the company's first performance appraisal program. During one of my own performance reviews, my past came back to life:

Them: *You're not a good project manager. But you have other qualities that interest us.*

Me: *Oh? Like what?*

Them: *Well, you listen. Nobody listens in corporate America. And people trust you. You don't reposition your opinion when senior management's in the room.*
We're spending hundreds of thousands of dollars to send our executives to listen to management gurus, and you know what they say when they come back?

Me: *No, what?*

Them: *That these guys all sound like Kenny Moore.*

So, that's how I ended up as corporate ombudsman. I still do priestly work. I represent the corporate common good. I'm a conduit between senior management and the concerns of 13,000 employees. I deal with problems of trust, belief, and caring. In my monastic days, we referred to this quandary as a crisis of Faith, Hope and Charity. I've discovered that the problems confronting business leaders are not only fiscal, they are also spiritual.

"And my own journey — through corporate and economic changes, through cancer, through heart surgery, through raising two wonderful boys — has taught me that only the important things really matter. That's why I do less of everything else."

20

How to

Customize Training Programs: Getting What You Need

LESS•O•METERS

STEPS: 5

TAKEAWAY: Make everything pass your own smell test, and be the Poobah!

KEEPING SCORE: Stop going to one-third to third-quarters of what's been mandated

WHY DO LESS

Most corporate and outsourced training programs are designed around the organization's needs – not necessarily yours • And even the best-designed programs can be tailored to better meet your needs

HOW TO DO LESS

1

Ask yourself: "Why should I care?"

All training must pass your own smell test

Sure, we all need to invest in our own continuous improvement and education. But if you went through all the training you're supposed to, you'd be in training 29 hours a day! The first criteria for whether you will attend and commit your full self to any training should be yours, not the company's.

So don't ask why the *company* wants you to care — like learning the latest new product info or improving teamwork through mandated programs. The first filter you use should be why *you* should care. (The following are the three most popular examples of why you might care. See Chapter 19 for more)

- **Is work important to you, but less important than life?**
  Then you will want to do everything you can to get in and out of company-sponsored training as quickly as possible, with as little effort as possible. Yes, you want to learn. But you also know you have more important things to learn *outside* of the workplace, and you want as much time as possible for those opportunities.
- **Do you want to make a difference?**
  Where most of your work really matters?
  Then you will want to screen all company-sponsored training according to your own definition of What Matters — not the company's. What are the one, two, or three things you do in your job that make the most difference to the most people? You want to make sure you spend more time in training on those things than anything else.
- **Do you want to be the best you can be?**
  Then you will want to screen all training opportunities according to *your* focus, *this* year. What one or two things do you need to quickly learn so you can hone your competitive

edge over anyone else who does your job? You will need to be diligent in selecting which vital few opportunities get your full commitment and attention.

•

Create your own smell test by:

- **Reading the syllabus and training objectives**
  Always ask for a copy of these before attending any training session
- **Quizzing your manager, or the training's sponsor – before the training**
  Push past whatever's being promoted, to very pointed questions about how the training relates to your needs — as you've defined them. (For more about how to quiz your manager, see Chapter 17)
- **Quizzing the trainer**
  Same thing: Push past the advertised reasons for taking the training

2

Time to decide…

Does the training pass your smell test, or not?

Three possible answers…

2 a

"Yes, I really care about this training!"

Then skip to Step 4

2 b

"No way! This is going to be a total waste of time."

Then do everything you can to get out of this training!

Tell a white lie, be absent that day, arrange for a conflicting client meeting. Do anything you can to get out of it. Remember, you only get 1440 minutes every day. Do not collude with timebandits!

(For more about saying No, see Chapter 10)

2 C

"I have to go. Pressure is being applied..."

Then evoke your rights as Grand Poobah.

Take the *preventative* actions in Step 3 before moving on to the *proactive* actions in Step 4.

3

You are the Grand Poobah of your life.

Learn the training secret that all Poobahs know

I have *never* met a senior executive who accepted the amount of time he or she was asked to spend in training. *One hundred percent* believed that their time was more valuable than the value they would receive by attending a full-blown version of the training. *One hundred percent* requested, *and received*, the Executive-Summary-Cut-to-the-Chase version of the training. I have seen Can't-Deliver-In-Less-Than-Three-Days training somehow, miraculously, delivered in three hours. And it worked! All because that's all that the Poobah would sit for.

Is your time any less valuable? Of course not.

Evoke your rights as Grand Poobah.

Call the trainer. Ask how to get the condensed, executive summary version of the training.

Every training program that you will be asked to attend or go take online *always* has a Grand Poobah version! I absolutely guarantee it. (The trainer had to submit that version to get budget approval.)

Unless you are absolutely and passionately thirsting for what's in that training, *never* accept the full-blown version without first trying to negotiate for the Poobah version.

•

Those who have practiced this strategy have reduced their unwanted and/or mandated training time by 33% to 75%.[1]

(Whadda concept! You're helping your employer ensure that you can be more productive by wasting less time.)

The goal isn't merely to play hooky. It's recognizing that you only have X-hours per year to invest in your own development, and that you are responsible for freeing as many of those hours as possible for whatever training will make the most difference in your performance.

4

For better ("I really care about this training") or worse ("I *have* to be here"), you're about to head into training....

Before you attend the session or go online, write down three sentences.

Complete the following statements...

- "The one thing I absolutely must **know** from this training is..."
- "This is how I'm going to evaluate what the experience **feels like...**"
- "The one thing I must be able to do after completing this training is..."

Yep, it's your universal tool: Know, Feel, Do. (For more, see Chapter 3.)

4 a

Use Know, Feel, Do to be a proactive participant

Grill the instructor. Probe. Question. Push back. Debate. Until you get what you need. Any training you attend must be results-based. Not just as the company or the trainer has defined results. But as you define the outcomes that you need. The overwhelming majority of people who attend training are passive participants — waiting to be fed the specific things they need. All Poobahs (both senior execs and anyone who's proactive in their own development) listen and learn actively. They make sure they understand what they're going to learn, and probe for immediate, useful, and meaningful ways to apply it.

(For more, Chapters 5–13 offer tips in proactive participation — from asking "Why" up to five times, to CLEAR, to the criteria for any successful meeting or training event.)

5

Recognize that almost all training evaluations stink.

Most are smile-sheets that ask only rudimentary questions.

When the training is done:

Ask yourself three questions that almost never appear on any evaluation:

- **Did this training "connect the dots" for me?**

  You live in an interconnected world. Yet most every training program is designed to deliver isolated solutions. (Example: Sales training for the latest new product will almost certainly leave out your bonus structure, how to get additional coaching from your manager, and how to research what the competition is up to. Yet, all these things affect your sales success.) There's a good reason for this approach — to focus the training so it can be successful. But in the real world, nothing happens in isolation. To customize future training to meet your needs, you must either search for instructors and content that do a great job of connecting the dots, or string together your own custom-designed curriculum, where you've figured out which courses need to be interwoven.

- **Did this training make me uncomfortable and push my thinking?**

  Almost all training evaluations equate trainer likeability and easy-to-apply content with success. Yet the best, deepest, most meaningful learning often comes when we are pushed out of our comfort zones, made to feel a little uncomfortable, and forced to wrestle with deep issues. While discomfort should be kept limited and focused, make sure you evaluate all training in how and where it pushed you — and, in the future, string together new courses that will push you further.

- **Can I successfully apply what I've learned in the next 30 days?**

  Here's where easy-to-apply does come in! But raise the bar. Seek out just-in-time training opportunities, tools, and content.

Applying anything you've learned within 30 days is the *longest* timeframe you should accept. Ideally, it should be within 1–48 hours. And *successfully apply* means that you also got some coaching about how to deal with your manager in implementing what you've just learned. Because s/he will be one of your biggest allies or barriers.

While the answers to these questions may not change the training you just took, they will help you seek future training that best meets your needs.

WHAT'S BEHIND DOING LESS

Let's face it. **Training is a negotiated compromise.** We all need to invest heavily in our own development, but we have limited time to do so. Whether it's the company's money or our own, funds will always be less available than we would like. And while all training should be just-in-time, the realities of conflicting schedules and priorities often make that difficult.

Even in the best companies, with the best training, under the best of circumstances, you are going to have to *work the system* to ensure that most of those compromises are in your favor.

Every Poobah works the system. Like this anonymous advice from a leader who's been featured in several top business magazines: "If you want to customize training to meet your needs, order all the 'sanctioned' materials, so the organization thinks you're following the rules, then throw them out. Design what you know that you need. Do the right thing."

And this from the head of leadership development in a Fortune 100 company: "When I'm trying to push the envelope, I have two separate speakers and workshops at the same time — one who is traditional and conservative, and one who is cutting edge. All the conservative leaders, who would normally gripe about the other session, go to the traditional workshop and give it high marks. The others, who think outside the box, get exposure to new ideas and speakers that our company normally wouldn't sanction."

And from a high school principal: "Two superintendents ago, I had a boss who really pushed my thinking. I loved it. He set my wheels in motion. Since then, those wheels have been grinding to a halt. So a year ago, I did my own 360° survey — asking faculty and staff what I should work on. I got great feedback, and I developed my own training program. I'd take a workshop, then I'd teach what I learned. Then I'd take another workshop, then teach it. Within a year, I grew a lot."

•

No one but you knows how to design training for you

Proactive learners try to customize every training opportunity to best meet their needs. When that becomes impossible, or takes too much work, they string together different training events to meet those needs. Net-savvy learners do a lot of comparison shopping online. Others work through peer recommendations. Still others blow off in-house training, and instead make the case to their manager that it's worth it to send them to outside conferences, pay for a university class, or pick up the tab for an outside online offering. There is no one right way to pull together everything you need. But there is only one strategy if you want to be in charge of your own growth…

Customize training to meet your needs, not just company needs.

WANT MORE?

Side Trips

Speaking of pushing one's thinking, taking charge of a situation, and training that can be applied in a constantly changing world, how many of these have you read?

- *Ranger School, No Excuse Leadership,* by Brace Barber
- *The Republic,* by Plato
- *On War,* by Karl Von Clausewitz
- *Code of the Samurai,* by Yuzan Daidoji,
- *The Art of War,* by Sun Tzu

21

How to

Continuously Improve Your Do-Less Skills

LESS•O•METERS

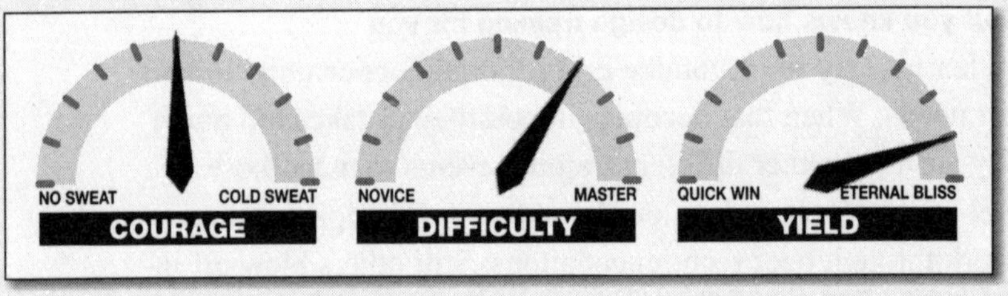

STEPS: 4

TAKEAWAY: The key skills all have to do with how you take in and share information

KEEPING SCORE: Create your own Do-Less School — assignments you seek out

WHY DO LESS

You've tried a few of these Do-Less tips, and they work • Great! • But how will you continually improve? Another career milestone is whether you seek assignments to propel your Do-Less skills to new levels

Pre-Work

Doing less, continuously, requires a variety of skills.

No one can master them all.

But three skills are more important than all the rest.

- Scanning, synthesizing, and clarifying information
- Advocacy
- User-centered communication

Before we move on to how-to's, here's what's behind each skill…

•

Scanning, synthesizing, clarifying

Your senses are assaulted on a daily basis. Everything and everybody wants your undivided attention. A universal skillset, for any worker in any industry on any project, is the ability to scan endless streams of information, synthesize it (separate out and ignore the "noise," focusing only on what's useful and valuable), and then clarify what that information means to a particular task or decision.

Few people have been trained to scan/synthesize/clarify, and do so *quickly*, *thoughtfully*, and *thoroughly*. Yet that's exactly what's required of all of us, tens to hundreds of times a day. Mastering this skill is your universal shut-off valve. It doesn't take you all the way to doing less, but it helps you reduce and focus the daily onslaught.

•

Advocacy

Some might call this skill selling, persuading, marketing, or presenting. Others might say it's facilitation or coaching, or deeply listening: confirming what's been heard, and promising to pass it on. Still others might call it managing up. Each description is partially right, yet falls short. You could hone all these skills and still miss a major component of advocacy — *courage*.

Advocacy is taking a stand on what you know is right. And doing so in ways that a) convince others, b) compel them to act, c) don't get you fired, and d) actually increase the respect others have for you.

Unfortunately, the number of workplaces and leaders who will help you build this skill is horrifyingly low. Yet build it you must, if you are going to continuously do less. Most everything in every workplace (including most managers) is specifically designed to get you to do more, not less. So you need to be able to take a stand, for yourself and for your teammates. Advocacy is the moment-of-truth skill in doing less. It's the skill that separates the Less Wannabe's from the Less Lifers.

•

User-centered communication

More than two-thirds of this book is about how you relate to others, connect with them, and share ideas with them. Why? Because the top sources of work complexity are *How We Communicate* and *Unclear Goals and Objectives*.[1] If you are not super clear, everyone around you does lots of unimportant, unfocused, and wasteful work. And that boomerangs back at you. Projects and decisions that you thought you'd gotten off your plate continuously come back for clarification, check-ins, course corrections, micro-management, and more.

User-centered communication goes beyond mere clarity. This skill is the heart, soul, and brains behind doing less. *User-centered* means…

- A higher standard of *empowerment:*
  You communicate so others can make more informed and independent decisions
- A higher standard of *respect:*
  You recognize that each time you communicate, you use a portion of someone's precious 1440 minutes
- A higher standard of *usefulness:*
  You organize and share what you know so others can quickly and easily put it to use

- A higher standard of *focus:*
  You are disciplined, diligent, and passionate about helping others focus on their "vital few"

•

If you are serious about continuously doing less, you'll dedicate yourself to honing these three skills.

HOW TO DO LESS

1

Seek out assignments that will take your scanning, synthesizing, clarifying skills to new levels

Ask your manager to help you find projects with short deadlines and steep learning curves, preferably with teammates from multiple disciplines. Projects like:

- Boiling the results of a six-month project down to a 15-minute presentation
- Writing the executive summary for a lengthy and complicated research project
- Interviewing customers or employees on thorny, controversial issues and preparing a senior executive presentation
- Examining gazillions of PowerPoint presentations and progress reports from a lengthy project, then based on what you uncover, recommending new, simpler ways, to communicate project progress
- Joining an ongoing, complicated project mid-stream, then forcing yourself to scan and understand all project documents in under one-half hour

If you already do these things, my condolences — I feel your pain. But you can set even higher standards. Like being able to juggle two or more of these kinds of projects at once. The goal is not masochism, but increased learning that can be applied elsewhere, like scanning emails, or running your own projects.

Watch out for jargon, buzzwords, and consultantese. Completely edit out, or fully explain these deadly viruses. Everybody uses them like they know what they really mean. Very few people do. Use everyday language. And stories.

❷

Seek out assignments that will take your advocacy skills to new levels

Again: Projects with short deadlines, steep learning curves, cross-functional teammates. Like:

- Representing the voice of the customer during a Corporate-driven initiative. Being relentless in how you push back from the customer's perspective
- Representing the voice of the employee during a Corporate-driven initiative. Being relentless in how you push back from the employee's perspective
- Surveying your team: How would they redesign the tools, processes, and information flows mandated by the company?
- Ignoring Corporate's plans for rolling out a new program to your team. Redesigning the roll-out from your teammates' perspective

•

How to be an advocate: Reread Chapters 10 – 13, and 17 – 18. Remember your desired outcomes: a) convincing others, b) compelling them to act, c) not getting fired, and d) increasing the respect others have for you.

❸ a

Seek out assignments that will take your user-centered communication skills to new levels

This is probably the *one skill* that needs the *most work* in the corporate world. Actively pursue assignments like:

- Reworking senior exec presentations to employees, ensuring that all language and examples are from the employee's perspective

- Reworking online worktools, employee intranets and portals, and project systems from the users' perspective — so they can quickly access the information they need, and ensuring that it's organized and delivered the way they say they need it
- Partnering with Corporate Communications on a major project to ensure your teammates get information they can use, that's designed around their needs

3 b

Redesign your company's 360° feedback on communication. Hold yourself and your team to a CLEAR standard

Most corporate-driven communication surveys are unbelievably wimpy. Truly user-centered communication follows the CLEAR model. It includes or explains:

• **C**onnections	to the person's current projects or workload
• **L**ist next steps	What you want them to do
• **E**xpectations	What success looks like
• **A**bility	How they'll get things done: lists tools and support
• **R**eturn	Their WIIFM: explains "What's in it for me?"

(For more, see Chapter 5)

Evaluate how often you and your teammates cover these five points, and brainstorm ways to improve.

4

Repeat Steps 1 – 3, again and again

Continuously learning how to apply these skills to continuously do less.

WHAT'S BEHIND DOING LESS

Neal Sofian is CEO of The NewSof Group, a healthcare consulting firm. His team includes educational consultants, behavioral change experts, researchers, writers, and software programmers. Neal was recently brought in by a global pharmaceuticals firm to help them evaluate and simplify a project that will transform how that company delivers its products.

Where did Neal hone his clarifying/advocacy/user-centered skills? "Running Everyday People, a drug crisis center. I did crisis and suicide intervention, emergency housing, runaway youth counseling, drug and alcohol counseling. We were an anti-establishment service agency and proud of it. Our motto was, 'Hassle free help. No questions asked. No name needed. Nothing to sign.'"

Dr. Charlie Kreitzberg is CEO of Cognetics, a leader in the design of user-centered software. He's also editor in chief for *User Experience* magazine, and a director in the Society of Information Management. Where did Charlie hone his clarifying/advocacy/user-centered skills? "Working on an early version of hypertext, which is the way people jump from one thing to another in online environments. Studying the way people followed links, and why, and how, taught me how little we all knew about what users really need, and how much we had to learn to get it right."

I worked on my own Do-Less skills under a college professor, Conrad Bruckman, who was compulsive about "form follows function." And under a cherished mentor, Lou Silverstein, a design director and managing editor at the *New York Times*. I was never more than a foot into Lou's office before he grabbed his soft, thick pencil — the kind kids use in kindergarten — so he could rework whatever I'd hand him. At the time, both men really ticked me off with their attention to detail. Now, I'm forever thankful.

The point is…There is no Do-Less School. Just experiences you create for yourself, the passionate service of others, and mentors who will hold you accountable to higher standards.

Oh, the places you'll go if you seek out those assignments and those mentors. You'll constantly discover new ways to blow stuff off! You'll become a Pushback Zealot.

WANT MORE?

Clarifying/Advocacy/User-Centered Starter Kit

- *The Design of Everyday Things,* by Donald Norman
- *Don't Make Me Think,* by Steve Krug
- *The Inmates Are Running the Asylum,* by Alan Cooper
- *Envisioning Information,* by Edward Tufte
- *Conversationally Speaking,* by Alan Garner

22

How to

Deal with the Stupidity of Performance Appraisals

LESS•O•METERS

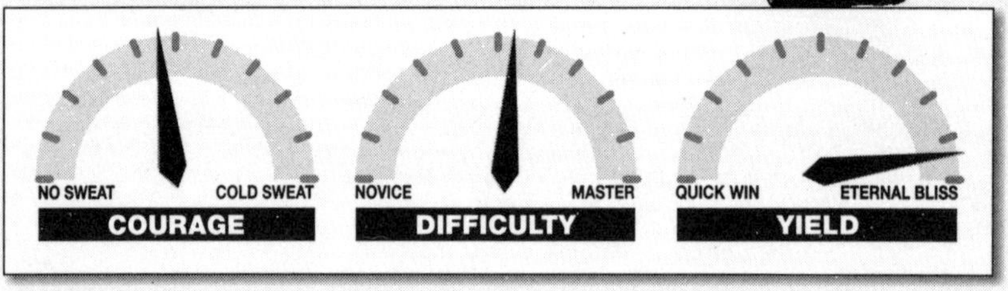

STEPS: 2

TAKEAWAY: Focus on what you can control — all the rest is just noise

KEEPING SCORE: By ignoring more, you can actually earn *higher* appraisals

WHY DO LESS

In most companies, the performance appraisal game is just like Vegas — the house wins more, and more often, than you

Pre-Work

Performance appraisals themselves aren't stupid. Getting good feedback on your work is always important.

What makes them stupid is how over-engineered and under-supported the entire process is in most companies. And the way the appraisal process typically plays out, there's a built-in flaw that will never be resolved: most managers do not like playing God — making judgments about someone else's worth, and being extremely candid with tough-love feedback.

HOW TO DO LESS

1

Understand how and why the game is played

Companies say that their appraisal process is focused solely on your *performance*, yet every manager knows that what he's really doing is determining how much *money* you're going to make.

Also, in most companies, there isn't enough time allowed for meaningful back-and-forth at the beginning of the process — ("The company says I have to turn in your goals for next year. So, can you tell me what you think they should be by tomorrow?") — and so little time for meaningful back-and-forth throughout the year, that your appraisal process is more like a paint-by-numbers exercise than most senior execs will ever admit.

Further, most managers don't get the mentoring and development they need to perform deep, thoughtful, and meaningful appraisals. They get Corporate-driven checklists, deadlines, and pressure to check off the boxes. (Very few companies are willing to make the hefty investment in coaching and development that's required to help most managers overcome their concerns about playing God.)

•

The company's real goals are to:

Maximize control, minimize cost,
provide legal documentation to protect the company if you are ever a bad person...
NOT to give you meaningful feedback

Despite all that you've been told, your performance appraisal has several primary goals, and getting you the rewards you deserve is hardly among them:

- To identify the 10%-or-so of performers who might be groomed for leadership positions
- To identify the 15%-or-so of performers who should be fired
- To provide legal documentation on how the company handled the process of letting those people go
- To manage and control compensation costs for the people who cost the company the most money — the remaining 75%
- To control how everyone stays focused on the goals set by senior management

This part works!

•

The rest falls way short....

Most every study ever done shows that the performance appraisal process is rife with flaws, such as inadequate training, and is usually poorly implemented. (All true.) But these studies assume that the goal of performance evaluations is to get you a fair and meaningful assessment, as well as a fair and equitable reward for you. *That's not it at all.*

In most companies, the performance appraisal process is a highly functional control and budgeting tool. If you are part of the 75% masses — (who are not about to be fired, and won't ever get a key to the executive washroom) — it would cost your company too much time and money to truly understand how you get everything done everyday. (Really good appraisals, which are sometimes done of senior execs at big companies, include multiple layers of 360°

feedback on more than 50 different dimensions — like how you earn people's respect; how you build teams; how you inspire trust; how you develop people; how you delegate authority; how you think; etc.) So they build a process that gets them what they need: better control — how rigidly you focused on whatever they said would create revenues and cut costs. Maybe with a couple "soft" people measures thrown in. (But guess which measures — hard or soft — matter more!)

As far as rewards: Any truthful HR or compensation person can tell you how forced distributions and predetermined salary budgets have a lot more say in where monies go and how they're distributed than your performance review.

And don't believe that technology can take over the detail work of a performance assessment. One Fortune 50 executive rants about that myth: "I've been complaining to my boss about how our performance system has been dumbed down to the point of being worthless. The company just spent a ton of money redesigning the system so it's all automated — 'Click the box' and 'Enter comments, if you'd like' — rather than asking folks to talk to each other, and have open and honest dialogue. Now I feel like we're just going through the motions." The only performance assessments that really matter involve open and candid conversations, not checklists or rankings.

Whenever companies scrutinize how employees rank their boss, office politics often emerge. Tom, a senior manager at one of North America's leading restaurant chains, describes what can happen.

"We have a system here that ties our personal performance to the values of our company, using twelve questions from the Gallup Organization. We answer these questions anonymously, but in a small group, it's pretty easy to figure out who wrote what. Well, the scores are supposed to have an impact on our boss's performance appraisal. So she always pushes us to give her the highest score — (she wants her bosses to believe she exemplifies the company values) — or we get in hot water.

"This year, she got upset that her score fell slightly from last year. So all of us had to go to a class that explained the twelve questions in more detail. We already understood the questions! We just made the mistake of answering them truthfully."

The worst part of the horribly-flawed appraisal process has nothing to do with money, or fairness, or feedback, or people playing with the rankings to manage perceptions. (Which happens a lot!)

What makes it so unforgivably stupid is that it's just another task that overworked, overburdened employees have to perform. Another way to eat up your daily1440 minutes. Like you, Tom would have much preferred to be accomplishing something for the company and spending time with his family. Instead, he played the game, and continues to regret all that wasted time and energy.

So Step 1 is recognizing how flawed the game is, and deciding to work the game to your best advantage.

2

If you are being assessed:
Ignore all the blahblahblah that your manager throws at you
(she's just reading the company-provided script),
and concentrate only on three things...

2 a

Ask your manager at least monthly, if not weekly:
"How'm I doin'?"

Don't accept non-responses. (Like "Great. Keep doing what you're doing.") Push for specifics on the project-of-the-moment:

- *Have you heard back from Corporate on the schedule I put together? Did they say anything could be improved?*
- *I thought that meeting went really well. Is there something you would have changed?*
- *I know I could have handled that customer call better. What would you suggest for next time?*

Make this part of your ongoing dialogue with your boss, and not just an occasional check-in. If it's ongoing…

- **You'll know ahead of time whether or not she "gets it"**
  If she keeps giving you non-responses, she probably doesn't know how to assess your performance, which means it will be hard for her to effectively support your big raise or or promotion even if you are doing a terrific job. Knowing this means…
- **You can change things before it's too late**
  If you wait for your quarterly, semi-annual, or annual review, you'll have too little time to change what you're focused on, or seek help from others besides your manager
- **You'll know what to expect**
  If you've done those mini appraisals yourself, you have a fairly accurate read on how she's going to fill in those boxes
- **You're training her**
  You're being proactive and focusing her on the areas that will give you the best shot at a great appraisal
- **You're making her job easier**
  When she sits down to do your formal fill-in-the-boxes appraisal, you've jumpstarted her efforts with multiple mini performance appraisals

2 b

Ask your manager, at least every other month:

"Are these <u>still</u> the three things that are most important?"

A major flaw of almost all performance assessment processes is that they're static, while the work that you do changes every day. (In the Performance Assessment Pretend World, your goals are set at the beginning of the year. And then you're supposed to be focused on those goals for the entire year. In the real world, we know that's bogus. Change happens. Yet most assessment processes aren't built to accommodate dynamic real-world changes.) *Re-confirm your top three goals at least once every two months…*

- **So you know you're focused on what you'll be compensated on.** Try to get that list down to three things. Never more than five.
- **So you train your manager to pay attention to the disparity** between what was locked-in at the beginning of the year, and what was actually worked on

(For 2a and 2b: For more details about how to have these conversations, see Chapters 16 and 17)

2 C

Then:

Trust your gut and your own ethical compass when deciding which work really matters. Everything else is just noise

If you've done your homework in 2a and 2b — you're getting regular feedback on your performance and regular updates on the changing priorities sent down from above — and you're doing your best, you've done all that you can do to max out your assessment and your reward. All the rest; the forms, the scores, the meetings (like the silly follow-up training that Tom, our restaurant chain senior manager, had to attend), the additional projects, the last minute work to increase sales or cut costs — that's just noise aimed at getting greater control over budgets and implementation plans, that will have little or no effect on how well or poorly you will do personally.

Blow off as much of the noise as you can.

•

Everyone who followed this basic approach reported that

they were never adversely affected,

and often earned higher appraisals and higher bonuses.[1]

•

Why? Because they were more focused than their teammates. They did less jumping through hoops, and accomplished more. And that's really what performance is all about.

WHAT'S BEHIND DOING LESS

In January 2003, *Harvard Business Review* published a "Best of HBR" series — important thought-pieces that have stood the test of time. Among the articles was psychologist Harry Levinson's "Management by Whose Objectives?" first published more than three decades ago in 1970. He wrote:

"In ideal practice, [the process of measuring performance] occurs against a background of more frequent, even day-to-day, contacts and is separate from salary review. But in actual practice, there are many problems:

- No matter how detailed the job description, it is essentially static....However, the more complex the task and the more flexible the employee must be in it, the less any fixed statement of job elements will fit what that person does.
- With pre-established goals and descriptions, little weight can be given to the areas of discretion open to the individual but not incorporated into a job description or objectives.
- Most job descriptions are limited to what employees do in their [own] work. They do not adequately take into account the increasing interdependence of...[how the] employees' effectiveness depends on what other people do.
- The setting and evolution of objectives is done over too brief a time to provide for adequate interaction among different levels of an organization."[2]

Boy, did he nail it! Our interviews yielded almost identical comments about performance appraisals. If, for at least 30 years it's been no secret that the current approach is flawed, then why do so many companies still use it?

Because it's not really about appraising and rewarding performance, it's about control. I can personally attest to that.

During the recent economic downturn, several Fortune 500 firms asked me to help simplify their performance management, compensation, and appraisal processes. Each discussion started with how they needed to reduce costs by gaining more control over how bonuses were paid, or how they had too many performers who "Exceeded Expectations," which meant they needed to shift the bell-curve distribution, or how the senior leadership team needed to convince employees that they're now in a performance-driven culture. Not one addressed the issues raised by Levinson more than 30 years ago. And when I raised those issues, they clearly did not want to go there. (I walked away from all but one assignment.)

•

Appraisals are horribly broken and should be killed off.
Long live appraisals.

With all its built-in flaws, the performance appraisal process is probably going to be around for a long time. Unfortunately.

So focus on the portions of the process that you can control:

- Constant check-ins with your manager
- Trusting your gut and your ethical compass as to what really matters
- Doing your best

Everything else is just noise.

WANT MORE?

"Management by Whose Objectives?" by Harold Levinson, *Harvard Business Review*, reprinted January 2003

THE WAY OUT: EXECUTIVE COUNTER-MOVES

Finally admitting that performance assessments don't work does not mean that executives have to give up controls, or leave themselves open to undocumented legal situations, or feel like the inmates are running the asylum. **To reinvent this process** in a way that is helpful to everyone, including executives, please (I beg of you!), **see Chapters 29 and 30:** How to Turn Transparency Into an Advantage, and How to Fix Performance Management

QUOTES OF NOTE

Apart from documentation for legal purposes, the annual performance appraisal is a waste of time.
AUBREY DANIELS
Bringing Out the Best in People

Among the seven deadly diseases causing the decline of American industry: performance reviews and merit ratings
W. EDWARDS DEMING
Out of the Crisis

23

How to

Get Better Budgets with a Lot Less Effort

LESS•O•METERS

STEPS: 4

TAKEAWAY: Don't ask for money, ask for a second meeting

KEEPING SCORE: If you get that second meeting: 80% to 90% success rate

WHY DO LESS

Most everything you've been told about how budgets are set is baloney • Don't bother jumping through hoops to justify/quantify/rationalize/cut or supersize your numbers because you're playing with a stacked deck • (Stacked against you)

HOW TO DO LESS

❶

Do NOT focus on money

It's the very *last* thing you should discuss!

If you stay within the budgetary boundaries you've been handed (like "reducing costs by 10%"), or explain, in an oh-so-logical way, that your budget request is tied to the company's strategy, the game will always be rigged against you. Economic pressures in the marketplace are bearing down on your bosses. If you try these approaches, they have to say "no" because their job is to get you to produce more with less money. If you want more money, you'll need to think differently.

•

DO focus on the senior team's headaches.

Find out what's keeping the most senior members "awake at night."

You are searching for their *personal* needs and worries. Every senior exec, just like you, is a human being with very human foibles. S/he fears embarrassment, failure, or the inability to maintain perceptions. S/he craves reassurance, rewards, glory, or fame.

Here are some examples of what keeps a typical senior manager awake at night, and what that could mean to you:

- **Not meeting Plan,** after he's already told Wall Street he would. (His pain is intense. You can go for major bucks!…As long as your project delivers sales revenues within 90 days. Or if you use your budget to cut costs in *somebody else's* area, like helping Alpha Team cut *its* costs by 20%)
- **Losing control of a situation, or being surprised…Commonly linked to FUD: Fear, Uncertainty, and Doubt** (For most senior execs, this is HUGE! If your project promises insights into what's going on within the organization, with customers, or with

the competition, you can count on high-level support. This is exactly how many BigName consulting firms get their huge fees! They may talk about increasing revenue or cutting costs, but, in reality, what they're selling is an antidote to FUD: "We'll make sure you don't lose control, and aren't surprised.")

- **Scandal just rocked some other firm. Could it happen here?** (This worry can open up budgets for "soft" issues — like leadership development, training for front-line employees, or increased communications.)
- **How do I get employees to do more, and keep costs down?** (Go for budgets that connect the senior team with their employees — like company-wide meetings, increased communications efforts, and increased training budgets to help everyone better understand how to produce more.)

•

Discover what keeps <u>your</u> Grand Poobah awake at night. If you don't have regular access to the senior team, this will require some homework. Schedule some time with her lieutenants. Ask open-ended questions about what she's really worried about. Explain (even if it's a white lie) that you need to know this to better rally your troops. If you can't gain immediate access to lieutenants, look to their admin's. They know *everything!*

❷

Package the need for money to perfectly match the senior exec's very personal concerns

For example: "Making Plan is in danger unless we add two more people on this project for just six weeks." Or, "Our current performance management practices leave us open to a scandal." Or, "Without a budget to have engagement meetings, employee buy-in on your new initiative will be in serious jeopardy." Keys to packaging your pitch:

- **Do NOT** emphasize your department's needs, or even the strategic plan. Focus on the executive's *personal* agenda. Your goal is to make a connection with him as a person, not as a bank.
- **Remember** that you're addressing what *worries* him most.
- **Make that worry your headline and key message.** Like…
  Plan is in Danger.
  With two more people, for six weeks: Plan is out of danger.
- **Remember** that every budget request is about great dialogue between you and that executive. Do not *present*. Talk.

  (For complete details on packaging and presenting your pitch, see Chapter 6)

3

Your first budget meeting should last no more than 15 minutes

Make your pitch, but also make a favorable impression. The shorter the better. No handouts! Just you, and the key message. (What can you accomplish in 15 minutes or less? See Step 4.)

4

Closing your pitch:
DO NOT ask for money! Ask for another meeting

DO NOT submit your budget request during the first meeting. Do not mention any numbers in the first meeting. Your goal is to get invited back to a second meeting, where the exec is already predisposed to a request for more money — because s/he initiated and shaped the request!

•

If you are invited back to a second meeting,

you should have an 80% to 90% success rate in getting the budget you are requesting[1]

WHAT'S BEHIND DOING LESS

(...LESS JUSTIFYING, QUANTIFYING, RATIONALIZING, OR CUTTING YOUR BUDGET NUMBERS TO MEET EXECUTIVE EXPECTATIONS)

Three basic realities...

1. You need to look at your request from the approver's perspective. If you pursue a numbers-driven approach — logically connecting your request to whatever's in the strategic plan — the exchange isn't really about money. It's about risk-exposure. Approving your request for more money means that this executive has to explain that decision to somebody else. (To his bosses, or ultimately, to shareholders.) It will *always* be easier to shoot holes in your analysis and number-crunched logic, than it is for this executive to risk going over-budget.

However, if you approach your exec with an *emotional* argument, one that instantly resonates with what's keeping him up at night, he'll be more willing to stand by you. (Your budget is helping to cover his butt!)

A fact of life: The people who set budgets — great leaders and the very non-great — are people, with very human needs, wants, and desires. If you appeal to the best (and occasionally the worst) of those human traits, you'll get further than by resorting to rational, strategic planning-ese.

•

2. In a typical company with typical senior execs, the numbers in the strategic plan are a lot more arbitrary than you think.

Sure, strategic planning starts with satisfying customers, beating the competition, and a whole lot more. But businesses, like most anyplace, are political institutions. Politics drives an awful lot of the compromises that determine who gets what. Manager A gets more in his budget because the company doesn't want to lose him. Manager B gets more discretion in how she allocates monies because she has lots of political clout with the CEO.

Those compromises and politics determine your budget as much as any sacred Plan that's "written in stone." So jumping through hoops to over-explain how your request is aligned with the strategic plan, or cutting, cutting, cutting to meet some magical number that's been set before you, yields a lot less than you think it will.

•

3. It is an extremely rare leader who can separate his or her personal agenda from the budget and planning process. C'mon, we've all seen

COUNTER-POINT:

SENIOR EXECS AND HUMAN HISTORY HAVE THEIR SAY

Several senior executives read these suggested workarounds in draft-form. Every one had the same reaction, **"Why do you have to suggest that the only way to work with senior management is to use manipulation and guile? That's not how we think we work!"** Now, some of my best friends are senior execs, and they don't eat little kids for breakfast, they have tons of integrity, and they're actually quite nice! So, why does our research show that these workarounds — which may feel manipulative — are practiced by people who get the budgets they need?

•

Because, throughout human history in most of the world, budget-setting has never been about money or strategy. Setting budgets is about power, control, personalities, dreams, fantasies, revenge, pettiness, greed, caring, altruism, tithing, perception, sharing, fun, passion, vision, aspirations, discrimination, conflict, bartering, compromise, paybacks, payoffs, partnerships, and friendships — to name a few. Like work, budgets are personal. Even great business leaders with endless amounts of integrity cannot rewrite the law that says budgets are, and always will be, personal. The people who get the most money know this.

it. Whether it's the CEO's pet project-of-the-month; swanky offsites for executives while training budgets for everyone else are slashed; or executive compensation remaining steady while everyone else takes a pay-cut — once you get beyond the realm of the best-of-the-best leaders, personal agendas have a lot of sway in the budgeting process.

•

Don't get upset. Get even.

Understand how your budgeting system *really* works. Not how the strategic plan says it's *supposed* to work.

That's what I've learned from the masters of the game — mid-level and senior execs who know how to play the game to their advantage. Like Selim: "Listen, budgeting isn't really about numbers. It's about relationships, trust, and pain. If the boss trusts you to make his really big problems go away, you'll get more money. No matter how strapped the company is. No matter how much cost cutting is going on. If he is worried enough and if he trusts that you'll make that worry go away, you can write your own check."

And like Anne: "Sure, I jump through the hoops they want me to for our six-month budgeting process. I know the big boys love all that 'due diligence.' So I'm a good girl, and then I do my thing. Behind the scenes, I'm figuring out which executive has business challenges that match what I can deliver. I take him out to lunch. I ask questions about those challenges. I casually mention what my team is working on that might help. I follow up with him a couple times. Whaddyaknow… Come time to lock in the budgets, my buddy's in my corner, fighting for my piece of the pie." Anne's strategy is especially valuable in larger companies where decisions are made by committees. If that's your situation, you'll need to line up more than one buddy.

Masters like Selim and Anne know that if they can focus their first meeting(s) on whatever's bothering the person who controls the purse strings, *instead of focusing on the numbers* — eight to nine times out of ten, they get much or all of the budget they need.

Some classics plus a helpful new lens

- *Getting to Yes*, by Roger Fisher, et al.
- *Getting Past No*, by William Ury
- *You Can Negotiate Anything*, by Herb Cohen
- *How to Negotiate With Kids Even If You Think You Shouldn't*, by Scott Brown
- *How to Talk So Kids Will Listen and Listen So Kids Will Talk*, by Adele Faber, et al.

For More Money in Better Times

If we ever see those times again, when budget requests don't all end in convulsed laughter, try this approach. A senior vice president at a Fortune 50 company says that during the 1990s, it got him tens of millions of dollars on scores of budget requests.

1. **Have your team create their Wish List** for tools, training, and support services.
2. **Bid that list out,** as if you are going to purchase those items. Compile all the support documentation that your company's accounting wonks require.
3. **Write up a one-page — (no longer!) — Business Case for the purchase:** State the need or problem that this purchase will solve, the return on investment, costs, product description, vendor credentials, etc. Put the one-pager on top of the support documentation, and place it all in a folder.
4. **Be prepared for year-end:** Keep ten or more of these folders at the ready. About a month before year-end close, lots of execs will be scrambling to spend whatever is left in this year's budget so they can get at least that much again next year. And there you are: with ten or more budget requests fully organized, just needing a signature.
5. **Score big bucks!** Remember the First Law of Workplace Behavior: Make it easier for people do things your way, and you'll get your way more often. Make it easy for people to quickly spend their year-end stashes, and you'll get more of those stashes.

24

How to

Be a Trusted Advisor to Senior Execs

LESS•O•METERS

STEPS: 10 lessons

TAKEAWAY: Pick the 3 that work best in your situation

KEEPING SCORE: Getting in, behind those closed doors…and staying there

WHY DO LESS

You could take years to master the skills, and gain the wisdom of a sage and the patience of a saint

- Or…You could take a sneak peek at what goes on

behind those closed doors

HOW WE WENT BEHIND CLOSED DOORS

A panel of 15 senior vice presidents put together a list of the ten most important things to know about consulting with head honchos. These trusted *consiglieri's* all have at least ten years experience in coaching, coaxing, and the care-and-feeding of the executive suite in Fortune 250 companies. And all have been granted anonymity — they don't want their bosses to know they're sharing these secrets with you.

Ten Lessons from the Masters

❶

The stated problem is never the problem

- The perceived or stated problem is never the *whole* problem, and often not the *real* problem. Issues and challenges at the senior level are complicated, interconnected, and overlapping. And personality problems are often part of the mix. You will have to dig deep to get to the problem.
- Senior execs always have a personal perspective on major issues. That's one of the reasons for their success, and sometimes for their failure
- Play devil's advocate:
  Get everyone's assumptions in the open and on the table, including your own

❷

Data will set you free

(If it's used to tell a story or start a tough conversation)

- Data can create uncomfortable discussions. That's good.
- Be Switzerland: Detach from emotions and politics.
  Data are just facts and trends that leaders must figure out how to use
- When senior team behaviors need to change, or there's a lack

of alignment: feed them their own view of the world. Present data on how they assess themselves, and facilitate from a neutral position

3

Be proactive. Be opportunistic

- Get issues, ideas, and options on the table first
- Contract to do data gathering for them, so you get to see, understand, and deal with the data before anyone else does
- Help define the agenda. Literally. (Be the one who organizes the agenda for executive meetings, and facilitates those meetings. This creates opportunities to influence what gets discussed, and how decisions are made.)

4

Be a "pair of hands"

(Help with executive's day-to-day tasks and priorities, and be involved in delivering the exec's messages and plans throughout the organization.)

Gets you in – behind those closed doors

5

Consistent delivery on those priorities keeps you in

6

Never assume that what a senior executive just agreed to is ever complete and final

- The deal and the work always change. That's neither good nor bad. Just the way it is
- So be sure to check in with them constantly

7

Always take the high road. Always!

- Especially if alignment between senior team members breaks down, or politics grow: No matter how painful it gets, take the high road

- Tell the truth, take the blame, present bad news, whatever it takes. Always be able to look at yourself in the mirror

8

Be sure you know who the decision-maker is

- Decisions are only made by *one* person, *never* a team or committee
- Always get the *real* decision-maker to sign-off on what happens next. (That may be a different person from the one who is touted as the decision-maker. Some leaders let others sponsor and champion initiatives, but retain final-decision authority for themselves.)
- Beware of advocates, with their own agendas, masquerading as decision-makers
- Once you know who that decision-maker is, carefully observe the dynamics of meetings. Often, it's invaluable to sense when a premature "no" is about to happen, and get the topic off the table until the timing is right

9

Senior execs are savvy, smart, and not to be underestimated. Yet their directives often need to be clarified

- The more senior the executive, the more savvy they are. Never underestimate any executive, and always assume they know how to get what they need from you
- Most executives need to be forced to choose: Good, Fast, or Cheap? Get them to pick one, maybe two. *Never* all three. Nonetheless, they'll still believe they're going to get Good *and* Cheap *and* Fast. So be sure you repeat back to them, several times, the choice they made.

- Be part of the team that drafts how they communicate directives. This often clarifies the directive itself
- Sometimes, the best thing you can do is listen — intense and active listening. Waiting to ask the right questions until you've reflected on things can earn you immense respect

10

The best laid plans of mice and men...

WHAT'S BEHIND DOING LESS

"My boss is one of the smartest leaders in business today," says one *consiglieri*. "Smart enough to surround himself with bright people who help him be his best. As well as letting us know how to challenge him. The Top Ten list I wrote up is pretty much how we operate as a team. Kind of like **Guiding Principles for the Executive Suite**."

A good illustration of these principles in action is Xerox's recent turnaround. Incoming CEO Anne Mulcahy took the reins of a company that was $17.1 billion in debt, with only $154 million in cash. Yet by mid-2003, Xerox had $3 billion in cash and reduced debt by 21% — causing board member John Pepper to say, "I never thought I would be proud to have my name associated with this company again. I was wrong." What changed?

First, Anne Mulcahy brought a new approach to leadership, which, in turn, changed how her top lieutenants support her. "Part of [Mulcahy's] DNA is to tell you the good, the bad, and the ugly," says a colleague.[1] She is doggedly focused, and her advisors support her tough decision-making and fast action.

Another top advisor who contributed to this list isn't so lucky: "My boss has an ego the size of this building. I use these techniques to serve this leader, but not get caught up in his power plays and politics."

Is it possible then, for most of the lessons from the masters to play both ways — as guiding principles for advising leaders who "get it," as *well* as how to work with bad bosses?

Seems like it!

I sent this list on to 37 people who report to a CEO in big and small firms, in for-profit and nonprofit companies, or who serve senior teams as outside consultants. And the consensus was, yes, this list works both ways.

Says Ron, a management consultant and coach to some of business's biggest stars and notorious Bad Boys: "I use most of these techniques to help good leaders become great, and to protect myself and others from the bad leaders."

•

It's all about jumping through fewer hoops, and accomplishing more

- If you assume that **the stated problem is never the real problem,** you'll dig deeper in both questioning and advising senior execs — ensuring you get to what really needs to be done a lot quicker.
- **If you use data to tell a story or start a tough conversation,** you'll approach numbers-driven presentations a lot differently than you do now.
- If you know that **getting issues in front of them** before they do it to you will help you control your own workflow, you'll be more proactive.
- If you know that being a "pair of hands" will **get you into doors that are currently closed to you,** and that consistent delivery on those tasks will **keep you inside the executive suite,** you'll look for more opportunities to do so.
- If you know that **what they just agreed to is never complete and final,** you'll stop assuming that the strategic plan drives everything you do, and you'll touch base with those execs a lot more often.

- If you **always take the high road,** no matter what you're asked to do, you'll never lose yourself or your moral center in the push to deliver the numbers.
- If you **carefully define who the decision-maker is,** you'll be jumping though only one hoop, not many!
- If you always assume that **your senior exec is more savvy than you** (even when he isn't), you'll never underestimate him. And, if you always assume that his directives **need to be clarified,** you will always make executing those directives a whole lot easier.
- Finally, if you truly understand that the **best laid plans of mice and men** often go *kaflooey*, you'll be more willing to try to advise that exec to try something new.

WANT MORE?

Take an Advisor to lunch

You've got the list, now ask a top advisor how he or she applies it at your company. Based on what you hear, boil this list down to the Top Three that will work best for you, and start putting them to use.

25

How to
Measure Respect in a World of MoreBetterFaster

LESS•O•METERS

STEPS: 5

TAKEAWAY: Personal productivity: how hard or easy your company makes it to do great work

KEEPING SCORE: 6 new dimensions of respect

WHY DO LESS

No matter what happens in the economy, timeless issues like respect will always matter • That includes the design of your workflow and workload matter • Is your company doing all that it should to help you work smarter and faster? • Or is it making its control and inefficiencies part of your workload?

HOW TO DO LESS

1

Answer the six questions within the following...

	STRONGLY AGREE	AGREE	NEITHER AGREE / DISAGREE	DISAGREE	STRONGLY DISAGR
1. Competing on Clarity My manager organizes and shares information in ways that help me work smarter and faster	○	○	○	○	○
2. Navigation In my workplace, it is easy for me to find whomever or whatever I need to work smart enough, fast enough	○	○	○	○	○
3. Fulfillment of Basics In my workplace, it is easy to get what I need to get my work done — right information, right way, right amount	○	○	○	○	○
4. Usability In my workplace, corporate-built stuff* is easy to use (*Tools, training, instructions, information technology, etc.; all that is designed to help you do your work)	○	○	○	○	○
5. Speed In my workplace, that same corporate-built stuff gets me what I need, as fast as I need it	○	○	○	○	○
6. Time My company is respectful of my time and attention, and is focused on using it wisely and effectively	○	○	○	○	○

Emailable version:
www.simplerwork.com

SimplerWork Index™

Tracking the connections between great places to work and what it takes to do great w

Short Version: Full questionnaire, up to 50 questions • Developed by and copyright © The Jensen Group

2

Now, take a breath.

Answer:

What's the very first thing you thought about as you took this survey?

I've asked that question of thousands of people.

Typical reactions include:

- *I'm depressed*
- *Wow! My eyes have been opened. I've never thought about these things*
- *I'm pissed off about how my company treats me*
- *Ya know...If we got good at these things, we'd be so much more productive*
- *My boss doesn't want to hear about these things*

There is no right or wrong reaction. Whatever yours is, is. But be sure to take the time to remember that very first, from the gut, emotional reaction. There's a connection between the intensity of that first reaction and whether or not you'll do anything with the results of this survey.

3

Add up your score

(Strongly Agree or Agree = Favorable response)
(Disagree or Strongly Disagree = Unfavorable response)

•

Four or more Favorable responses: Congrats! You are in a great place to *work*: a place that is truly focused on helping you work smarter and faster. A place that is as concerned about your *personal* productivity and effectiveness, as it is about *organizational* productivity.
You needn't worry about Steps 4 – 5! Flip to another chapter.

•

Four or more Unfavorable responses: You are probably being dumped on. Your leaders are not only *not* doing all they can to help you be your best, it's entirely possible that they are passing their inefficiencies and control issues onto you.

(To compare your results to others, see sidebar)

4

From now on, for every assignment, every performance review, and job interview:

Keep asking your manager questions about how hard or easy your company makes it for you to do your best

It's like there's an Old Boy's Club for worrying about effectiveness, efficiency, and productivity, and you're not granted membership unless you're one of the Poobahs. That's bogus.

Many of the resources that your company uses are yours; your time, your knowledge, your energy, your passion, even your social connections. Since these are *your* resources, just like with anything else that's yours, you don't want them wasted, so you have to be careful about how they're spent.

Be relentless in questioning how easy or hard your company makes it to do your best. Use the SimplerWork survey as your starting point. (For more on using the Index in daily conversations, see questioning techniques in Chapters 5, 10, 11, 12, and 16)

The ultimate benefit to you is not whether any one company or manager treats you with more respect. This is about you raising your own standards. From this point forward, R-E-S-P-E-C-T includes *how* companies use the resources that you provide. The questions in this survey can help you create a more fully-informed picture.

Armed with that knowledge, you can decide how much, or little, to invest in your company.

5

Start sharing this survey, and everyone's responses, in every forum possible. With teammates, managers — everybody

The six survey questions relate to areas of personal productivity —

what your company is doing, or not doing, to help <u>*you*</u> do morebetterfaster every day.

Raising new productivity questions can change what gets measured inside your company. And that can change how your company helps you get stuff done.

•

Take a two-pronged approach to making this happen in your company:

- **Seek out leaders who will champion the use of the SimplerWork Index survey.** Look in human resources, performance management, and among leaders with operational responsibilities — like division executives or plant managers. Eventually, if not at first, they *will* sponsor your efforts. Why? Because improving the scores on each of the six dimensions of the SimplerWork Index helps you get more done in a day. And that's what *they* are measured on! So enlist them to track survey results within your team, and then share those measures up the chain of command.
- **Don't wait for those champions.** Create grassroots, bottom-up pressure. Share your survey results in professional organizations, or with teammates in other parts of the company. Talk about what you've learned since you began focusing on these dimensions of respect. Tell stories about how you are using your time and energy differently. Business is only in the earliest stage of understanding and tracking personal productivity. Economic pressures and the war for talent will eventually force every company to focus on these dimensions, but you can't afford to wait that long!

•

Your goal is to shine a light on an aspect of productivity that lies mostly in darkness — how easy or hard companies make it for you to do your best and produce morebetterfaster every day.

WHAT'S BEHIND DOING LESS

First, I need to mention what's *missing* from this chapter. Decent pay, appropriate benefits, great culture, being treated fairly with open and honest communication, and much more are still important dimensions of respect. And always will be. Keep focusing on them.

But they're no longer enough. We need to expand our view of what it means to be treated respectfully.

•

Profits v. People: Both sides have missed something

Throughout our *Search for a Simpler Way* study, we noticed a persistent problem in the ongoing People v. Profits debate. The results-driven Profits People constantly focus on delivering the numbers with an occasional, "Oh, yeah, our employees are our greatest asset." And the People People get all warm-and-fuzzy, saying "You'll get better results if your employees are happy and feel respected." Of course, both sides are right. And they've both overlooked something.

Companies get a return on your assets — your time, attention, ideas, knowledge, passion, energy, and social networks — in the form of profits. Yet, what kind of return are *you* getting for your assets: Is it getting easier to make a big impact at your company? How much of your time is spent doing great and important work? In your company, how much and how fast are you able to learn? How challenging, rewarding, and exciting is your work? If you invested your assets in another employer, would you get a better return?

We discovered that neither the People People nor the Profits People were treating employees as investors. Consequently, neither side talked about how employee assets, like time, were being invested. Or how those assets were being wasted. That discovery helped shape the SimplerWork Index. We began to explore how companies treat your assets. (See sidebar for results to date.)

•

New Views of Respect: By the Numbers

- **1992 to 1999:** In developing the Index, we borrowed from the world of consumerism, where respect's impact on the bottom-line had already been proven. When businesses want to sell you something, they work hard at perfecting how they treat you in areas of Clarity/Navigation/Fulfillment/Usability/Speed/and Time. Because all consumer research shows that you will buy more, and stay as a loyal customer if they get those things right!
- **Surveyed 10,000 individuals** in more than 400 companies. Results to date:

Four or more Unfavorable: 67%
Four or more Favorable: 19%

Competing on Clarity
Evaluates manager's effectiveness in helping individual work smarter and faster
48% favorable

Navigation
Evaluates company's effectiveness in helping individual find who or what s/he needs
28% favorable

Fulfillment of Basics
Evaluates company's effectiveness in work-oriented communication and knowledge mgmt
25% favorable

Usability
Evaluates company's effectiveness in all that it designs to help people get tasks done
19% favorable

Speed
Evaluates company's effectiveness in enabling employees to work in a 24/7, ever-faster world
14% favorable

Time
Evaluates company's respect for employees' time as an asset to be invested
12% favorable

Statistics on site, www.simplerwork.com, may differ. Participation at the site is self-selected, under uncontrolled conditions

What each measure means to you

Favorable scores mean that it's easier for you to do your best. Depending on your job, you may wish to focus on one measure more than the others…

- **Competing on clarity** seems to matter most to people whose daily, operational success is directly tied to the effectiveness of their manager
- **Easy navigation** seems to matter most to those who work in ad hoc or virtual teams, or who are fairly empowered by, and independent from, their manager
- **Great fulfillment of basics** matters most in hierarchical organizations and in process-driven functions, such as research

So What?

What do the Index results mean? If you are an executive in a large company (entrepreneurial environments fare much better) with 100 employees…

52 have to go back to their manager again and again to figure out what they're supposed to do

72 can't find what they need to do their best

75 are filling in the blanks for themselves on task/goal-communication

81 think their son's Xbox works better than the tools you supply

86 think you are email when it comes pushing speed down the chain of command, and snailmail when it comes to acting on employee feedback

88 have been trained by the company to guard their time, or at least to be dubious and have second thoughts or hang back, when asked to give more of it or manufacturing or sales — where your information needs are highly structured

- **Great usability** matters most to those whose daily tasks and efficiencies are intertwined with the effectiveness or inefficiencies of company tools such as intranets, handheld computers, or records-keeping
- **Speedy responses to your needs** matters most to those who receive constant top-down pressures to perform, but whose performance is dictated by how quickly the company provides them with what they need to do their job. That could mean approvals of your requests, responses to your questions — how your company reacts whenever you say "Here's what I need to do what you're asking of me."
- **Respectful use of time** seems to matter most to everyone! (Usually, survey respondents pick time *and* one of the others as mattering most.)

•

Why should the Profits People care?

Where's the bottom line impact?

Very simple: If your boss makes it easier for you to find what you need, easier for you to get answers, easier for you to use your tools, and if the company uses your time more effectively, they can ask you to do even more than you do today! Yes, they're being more respectful of you, but they're also getting better resource utilization. That has direct bottom line impact!

•

Nobody's the bad guy.

We're all the bad guy.

We all own part of the problem.

Ways to start…

Own the part of the problem that you can control: Like how you think about respect, and how much initiative you take on your own. Frankly, most employees can make their working lives better without saying squat to — or asking anything from — management. You can do more on your own, like:

- **Changing how you communicate:** How would others rank you on how well you compete on clarity or get them the right information in the right way at the right time?
- **Being a better simplifier and integrator:** How many times have you passed on lengthy documents, instructions, or corporate initiatives when you knew that all that your teammates needed was a tiny portion of what you sent?
- **Changing how you use people's time:** You create so many things — emails, teleconferences, meetings, documents — that use a portion of everyone's 1440 minutes. With each thing you create, are you doing all that you can to be respectful of people's time and attention?

•

Senior execs own the part of the problem that they control: If you are that executive, you must understand that the workload and pressures that employees feel, are driven, in large part, by what you build to help them get their work done. Yet who is holding you accountable for how well you do that? How are you being measured? Are you measured at all on how well you help each *individual* in the organization be productive, and not just on organizational productivity?

If you'd like to make changes, use what you learn from your survey results to…

- **Change leadership development programs:**
  For more, see Chapter 27
- **Change how you build infrastructure and worktools:**
  For more, see Chapter 28
- **Use information transparency as a competitive advantage:**
  For more, see Chapter 29

- **Reinvent performance management:**
  For more, see Chapter 30
- **Reinvent training and development:**
  For more, see Chapter 31
- **Evaluate organizational culture and ability to win the war for talent:**
  For more, see Chapter 32

•

Most important change:

Changing the debate

This index was developed in 1999 and has since been field-tested by a handful of leaders who "get" the First Law of Workplace Behavior: ease-of-use and reduced-use-of-time are *equal to — and sometimes more important than* — recognition, compassion, inclusion, rewards, penalties, loyalty, and hierarchy in their ability to drive human behaviors. These are leaders who realize that:

- To build better workplaces, we must first see how the design of work impacts the quality of our lives
- It is no longer acceptable to say that there's *work* and there's *life* and it's up to employees to balance the two. Every system, every process, every tool that a company puts in place uses a portion of your 1440 minutes. *Respect* now includes how well, or poorly, your company uses the finite time you have available every day.

What emerges out of this realization is a new kind of dialogue where respect for your time becomes as important to leaders as diversity, or safety, or working conditions, or global and generational differences, or career development paths. Those things are *now* important to business leaders, but they didn't start out that way. Most leaders weren't paying attention to those issues until the population at large started focusing on them.

Personal productivity will become important when enough of us tell our leaders it's important.

Leadership Lessons in Doing Less

Your Own Story

Think Like a Customer (Not a Manager or an Employee)

For a moment, stop thinking like a manager, and think about a recent shopping experience-from-hell or the most outrageously wonderful moment you've had in a store. Call upon your own passions *as a consumer*.

Let's say you wanted to buy a sweater. If the store didn't stock what you wanted, would you hang around — for years — waiting for them to meet your needs? Of course not. If the cash register didn't work, would you say, "That's OK. I understand. It must be hard to build an infrastructure and tools that meet my needs"? Of course not. If everything in the store was designed to minimize the retailer's attention to your needs, while maximizing their profits, would you partner with them in that effort?

Of course not. You'd *dis* the retailer. You'd never buy from them again. You might even go public with what you know, so that others wouldn't be mistreated like you.

A lot of what goes wrong has to do with simplicity: How easy it is to get the sweater... How easy it is to get answers to your questions... How your needs are designed into the sales process... How focused the company is on using your time wisely and effectively.

The SimplerWork Index merely translates consumer measures of respect — Clarity, Navigation, Fulfillment, Usability, Speed, and Time — into the world of the workplace.

In most companies, everything is designed to maximize profits and minimize the firm's attention to an individual employee's needs. Why is it OK for an employer to do that, but not a retailer? When it's hard to get answers to questions, or the corporate infrastructure stinks, or the training and tools we get are insufficient, why do we willingly suck it up?

If your goal is to lead the way to truly simpler work, you're going to need to recall moments where you demanded the respect you deserved. It can be as mundane as being a customer — "I want satisfaction, now!" — or any other moment in your life when you simply would not rest until things got better.

The secret to getting that kind of respect in the workplace is to think like a customer, not a manager or employee. Harness the fire-in-the-belly energy from the last time you were a customer scorned. (Or when you were goose-pimply delighted.)

If you'd do it for a sweater, why not for your career?

WANT MORE?

Go to www.simplerwork.com for an emailable version of the SimplerWork Index

26

How to

Decide: Stay or Go? How Much Is Too Much?

LESS•O•METERS

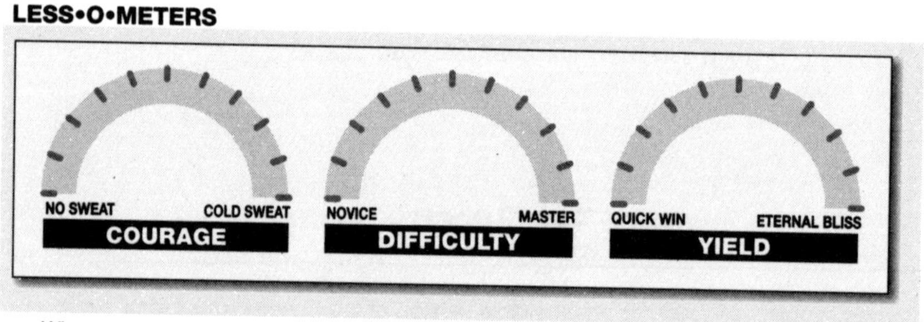

Where are you now?
Where do you want to be?

Where are you now?
Where do you want to be?

Where are you now?
Where do you want to be?

DRAW YOUR OWN LESS•O•METER NEEDLES

Now, it's time for you to decide what it takes to make your Stay/Go decision

- No one can do it for you
- Maybe use a pencil, so you can change your mind
- Maybe mark the date so you can track your commitment to yourself
- Remember, it is your life, your happiness
- Are you using your 1440 minutes wisely, and are they being respected?

Time to choose…Stay or go?

Pre-Work

Include the usual factors for deciding to stay or go:

Your manager's skills and attitude, your pay, your benefits, the economy, your own growth, happiness, and excitement, and more….

HOW TO DO LESS

1

Now, add new filters, new crap-catchers, new shut-off valves...

•

Delete more emails and run away from more meetings.
Stay if your manager and company support your efforts.
Go if they don't.

•

Set higher standards for information sharing and communication. Push to get more of the information you need, the way you need it, in order to make fully-informed decisions.
Stay if your manager and company support your efforts.
Go if they don't.

•

Set higher standards for how you and your teammates organize and share what you know. And coach teammates who unknowingly pass on too much of their own to-do list.
Stay connected with, and learn from, and laugh with teammates who get it.
Go elsewhere if they don't.

•

Change the way you interact with senior execs — one page summaries, helping them make better decisions, connecting with them as people and not as banks or strategists.
Stay if your leaders get it.
Go if they don't.

Learn how to say “no” in most any situation.
Stay if, more often than not, your decision is respected and enhances your career.
Go if it isn’t and doesn’t.

•

Learn how to question why you’re getting the workload you’re getting, and accept less of the party line and corporate spin.
Stay if, more often than not, your questions are answered truthfully and with integrity.
Go if they are not.

•

Learn how to deal with bosses who just don’t get it, or who pile on too much.
Stay if your solutions work and are appreciated.
Go if they don’t and aren’t.

•

Learn how to research and ask tougher questions about how hard or easy your company makes it for you to do your best.
Stay if you like what you discover.
Go if you don’t.

•

Learn how to track your own success in doing less, and continuously improve your do-less skills.
Stay if you’re doing less, and that works for your company.
Go if you aren’t and it doesn’t.

•

Learn how to address the stupidity of some corporate structures, and help your company measure respect in completely new ways.
Stay if your leaders get it, and are trying.
Go if they don’t and won’t.

•

All that comes down to just one thing...

Really grasp how precious your daily 1440 minutes are.
And learn how to respect other people's 1440 minutes.
Stay if the people around you also embrace this idea, helping you and others do their best.
Go if they don't.

Leadership Lessons in Doing Less

One Executive's Story... Everyone's Story

Stay or Go? Doing Less Reveals Character

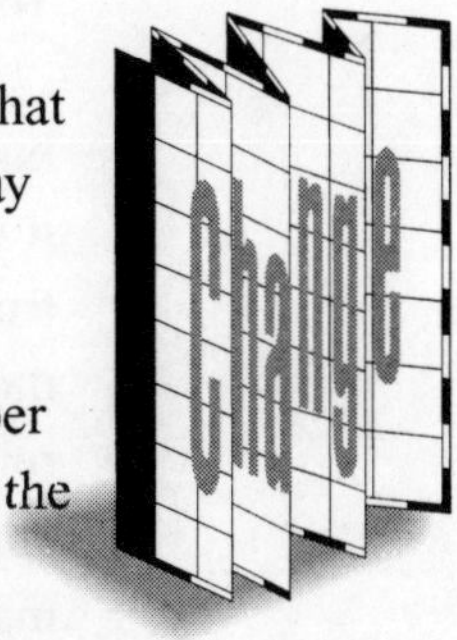

It has been said that adversity does not build character, it reveals what was always there. The same applies to the ability to stand up and say that it's time to do less with more. I learned this first-hand from a woman I met on a plane.

I was flying from Los Angeles to New York. It was mid-October 2001, only a month after the events of September 11. As I boarded the plane, I looked up and down the aisle. Most everyone's faces told a single story: the tension and fear of flying was still very real. My seatmate was a senior executive at a Fortune 100 company. Throughout much of 2002, her CEO would be lauded in the press for his ability to execute strategies during tough times. She held a slightly different view. In her words, she was pissed-as-hell at him.

There had been major changes at her company. New leaders had assumed new positions, and she was headed for a big social and team-building event at corporate headquarters. She really didn't want to fly to this event at this time. She offered all kinds of alternative solutions:

teleconferencing in, arranging for one-on-ones with key players, and more. The word back: show up in person. One more offsite she had to attend.

At one point, while she relayed this story to me, her eyes filled with tears. "What if something happens on this plane?" she asked. "I've got two daughters — four and six years old. What message am I sending to them? That work is about sucking up and doing what you're *supposed to do*, regardless of your personal priorities?"

What struck me about our conversation was not the outpouring of emotion. She just blurted out what many of us were probably feeling.

What got to me was her feeling of complete loss of control. Here's this woman at the top of the heap, probably making gazillions of dollars — (she was slumming next to me only because a corporate jet was unavailable). And yet she felt like she couldn't say "no." Whoa. If she can't take control of her life, how could us peons do it?

In the months that followed, we remained email and phone buddies. I did little more than provide a safe zone for venting. But it was clear that the dilemma she faced in that situation revealed her true character as a leader. She decided to dedicate herself to saying no more often, and having the courage to do less. That changed her relationships with the people she led, and they, in turn, felt more confident about revealing their true selves, which changed how they managed others. And, as she began to haul less baggage home from work, she was better able to enjoy her relationship with her daughters and her husband.

However, the CEO at her company sees things rather differently — he's not thrilled with this newfound freedom to say no more often — and so she's decided to leave.

I do not know how her story will end. But her example taught me an enduring lesson about leadership:

The true depth of a leader's character is fully revealed when that leader must make a choice between doing less or doing more.

3

Leader Essentials

What must leaders do to create simpler companies — workplaces where it's easier to do great work?

- Where it's easier for every individual to succeed?

If you want to create that kind of workplace, we've compiled several Top Ten lists of leader essentials.

In the first part of each list are **classic essentials** • Things that have always been important, and are becoming more so • Work on these fundamentals with ever-increasing diligence — your best talent will go (or stay) where they find these things

The remaining Top Ten items are emerging twenty-first century trends • Ways to go beyond the current best practices, and start creating workplaces where **every individual is as efficient, effective,** and **productive** as they can be and more people feel they are making a difference

27

How to
Fix Leadership Development

WHY IT NEEDS FIXING

Most executives are like everyone else — people who want to do the right thing and make a difference. And like everyone else, they need support to stay focused, cut through the clutter, manage complexity, and compete in a world of morebetterfaster.

Ten Essentials for Simpler Companies

Develop leaders who can do less and accomplish more

THE CLASSICS

Always been important…and becoming more so

❶

Develop the whole person:
Emotionally, intellectually, spiritually, creatively, and more

Maintain a robust and rigorous leadership development regimen. Here's a good start: the following is a list of leadership skills from three *Best Place to Work* companies, two leading nonprofit organizations, and one special forces unit of the U.S. military. A good development program identifies the leadership skills that need improvement, and helps leaders work on them.

Drives for Results

Maintains constant customer focus

Thinks broadly, and connects people to the vision

Creates new standards:

Constantly raises the threshold for performance possibilities

Is a change agent: Empowered and empowering

Is action-oriented

Is competitive

Makes tough decisions

Stays focused:

Knows how to decide what is important, and say no to everything else

Sets the vision, framework, and ways of thinking

Builds Winning Teams

Attracts the best talent: Promotes, selects the best people

Delegates authority

Leverages the entire organization:

seeks the best ideas and contributions

Provides air cover for risk-takers

Earns Respect and Respects Others

Is a servant leader: Removes any and all barriers

Takes a stand: On issues, values, and for others

Inspires Trust and Is Trusted

Openly shares information, with complete honesty and integrity

Maintains composure in time of crisis

Delivers what is promised

Acknowledges mistakes and limitations

Deflects credit to others

Encourages truth-telling, is approachable

Communicates Effectively

Engages everyone in vision, mission, and values

Creates common language and understanding between teams of people

Ensures everyone understands plans, goals, roles, and accountabilities

Valued Coach and Mentor

Provides timely, clear, candid, even-handed, and fair feedback

Listens

Rewards performance

Promotes meritocracy

Develops people to accelerate their development

Valued Citizen and Community Member

Values local, global, and environmental concerns

Values people with diverse backgrounds, experiences, and capabilities

Sets an example for volunteerism and giving back

2

Continuously enhance listening skills

Listening — really listening — is one of most leaders' biggest weakness

3

Continuously enhance communication skills

Use storytelling to engage people's hearts, minds, and souls

4

Develop enhanced skills for self-management

Know your strengths: Most people think they know what they're good at, and most people are wrong

- Don't waste time on areas of low competence – concentrate on your strengths
- Work to overcome your bad habits, and your own biases and arrogance

Know how you perform: Improve the ways in which you do your best

- Do you process ideas and information more quickly by reading or by listening to others?
- Do you perform best as a decision-maker or advisor?
- Do you function well under stress, or do you need highly predictable situations?

Know your values

Know where you belong: Most successful careers are not planned.
Know how to choose among opportunities when they present themselves, based on where you truly belong.

Know what you should contribute:
How will you know that you made a difference within 12 to 18 months?

Source: Adapted from Peter Drucker, "Managing Oneself," *Harvard Business Review*

5

Practice principles-based leadership

Live by your principles.
Be guided by those principles to make hard decisions. Support, coach, and mentor your peers in practicing principle-based leadership.
And make hard decisions about those around you who are not living by the organization's principles.

THE NEW ESSENTIALS

Developing leaders who will ensure that every individual is as efficient, effective, and productive as they can be

6

Constantly debate and examine the question, "What is a leader's accountability for life's precious assets?"

Every directive, and every system, process, tool, and structure that your company puts in place, use a portion of each employee's daily 1440 minutes. How accountable should you be for how your company uses, wastes, or enriches an individual's time? How does it change what you build, how you build it, and what you ask people to do in the name of corporate growth and sacrifice? There is a co-accountability between worker and leader. Both are responsible for stewardship of assets. Yet, leaders don't talk much about how they use people's time.

7

Reinvent your leadership university

Old model: Leaders talking to other leaders or instructors or gurus. New model: Customers and frontline employees are in the pit along with executives, guiding them into a new understanding of real-world implementation issues. Everyone is granted permission to go beyond questioning, into advocacy and tough-love feedback. The best executive mentors, coaches, and change agents are your own employees and customers.

8

Get your fingernails dirty, regularly

At least once a week, David Neeleman, CEO of JetBlue is called "Snack Boy," because he's in a plane picking up the trash and serving customers their snacks. Great role model! But to ensure your employees are as efficient, effective, and productive as they can be, you'll need to go further. Senior execs should be using their own company's cash registers, or customer service call centers, or help desks, or employee portals, or training manuals, or laptops on a regular basis. Since employees' biggest barriers are often the very systems and tools that have been built for them, senior execs should regularly experience those barriers. That'll get 'em fixed a lot faster!

9

Reinvent development assignments

Current career paths for up-and-coming executives include international assignments and responsibilities in different functions or business units. Great start! But to ensure they fully understand the work of work, developing execs also need additional stints as the Fool (counsel to the senior team, there solely to speak the truth to power), as the New Quant Person (focused on work-design and work-efficiency data), and as the New People Person (focused on developing user-centered tools and processes). These unofficial positions are great ways for leaders to understand the real implementation issues, and how to bring out the best in everyone in the organization.

⓾

Seek two mentors:

One half your age, one twice your age

For the next ten to fifteen years, two colliding forces are going to rock every leader's world: huge numbers of baby boomers will be retiring, but not really leaving the job market (creating new and unique pressures on healthcare, contract-work, and pension funds), *at the same time* that an equal number of Generation Y (currently 23 and younger) are entering as first-time employees (with completely different standards for information sharing that most execs are used to). Seek mentors to coach you through the intensity and meaning of these colliding forces.

28

How to
Fix Your Worktools

WHY THEY NEED FIXING

Tools help us deal with the ever-increasing complexity of work. Yet most corporate infrastructures, tools, and processes are designed to make things simpler for the company, not necessarily for the individual. If we want everyone to produce morebetterfaster, business must learn to be user-centered — working backwards from the needs of the people who do the work.

Ten Essentials for Simpler Companies

Develop worktools that help everyone do less and accomplish more

THE CLASSICS

Always been important...and becoming more so

❶

Build great organizational productivity tools

The right ones help execs track and manage the output of the organization; from budgeting and financial tracking tools, to project management tools, to supply chain, and resource allocation tools, to organizational structures and more. Be sure you're measuring the right things — for the right reasons.

❷

Build great personal worktools and spaces

Help every employee do their job more efficiently and effectively; Give the same attention to cubicles and conference rooms as you do to databases, training and development, processes and procedures.

❸

Build great connecting, collaborating, and learning tools and spaces

Not long ago, email replaced phone calls as the killer app. And now, every company is building better and more integrated ways for people to connect with one another. Human beings are intensely social animals — that's how we get things done. That's how we learn.

THE NEW ESSENTIALS

The majority of today's tools are company-centered — they were designed and purchased so executives could manage company resources more efficiently and effectively. That's good! But not good enough! Start examining management tools (like strategic plans, and budgeting and reporting documents), worktools (like databases, plans, and laptops), and collaboration and learning tools (like intranet spaces) from the employee's perspective.

Measure, track, and continuously improve all tools and processes based upon:

❹

Clarity

How easy is it for employees to share the information in those tools with common understanding and meaning

5

Navigation

How easy is it for employees to find whomever or whatever they need to work smarter and faster

6

Fulfillment of Basics

How easy is it for employees to get the right information they need, in the right way, in the right amount

7

Usability

How user-centered your worktools and processes are

8

Speed

How quickly corporate-built tools and processes get employees what they need, when they need it

9

Time

Do corporate-built infrastructure and processes treat each employee's time and attention as assets to be managed wisely, and not wasted

See Chapter 25 for more details about Clarity, Navigation, et al.

10

Create a culture focused on personal productivity

We are passing through a technological barrier as we develop new ways to collect data on how every individual performs his or her job. The only question that remains is *How will companies use this capability?* Will it be to enforce more control over each person? Or will it enable companies to take a more holistic view of each worker's needs — helping each one do their best?

For more, see Chapters 29 and 30

29

How to
Turn Transparency Into an Advantage

THREAT OR OPPORTUNITY?

Transparency — giving parties outside the company, like shareholders and customers, greater access to numbers and decisions made inside the company — has been thrust upon firms by accounting scandals. Yet the real power of transparency is *within* the company: giving more people access to customer data, performance data, decision-making processes, and much, much more.

Leaders now face a choice:

Is a world with no secrets a threat, or an opportunity?

Ten Essentials for Simpler Companies

Transparency provides a means for doing less and accomplishing more

THE CLASSICS

Always been important…and becoming more so

1

Communicate…

2

Communicate...

3

Communicate

Telling your story consistently and effectively is crucial. However, no communication plan is going to get everybody what they need, when they need it, how they need it.

THE NEW ESSENTIALS

Ways to leverage transparency so every individual can be as efficient, effective, and productive as they can be.

•

The idea is pretty simple: give all people all the information they need so they can better manage themselves, and make more decisions that ought to be part of their job. But leveraging transparency in ways that leaders can trust all this new openness and self-management — well, yeah, that can get a little complicated.

4

Build digital dashboards

When GE's vice chairman wanted a digital dashboard (continuously updated online information about the company's vital stats), he asked John Seral, chief information officer of the Plastics division, to take on the task. Within 120 days, 300 managers across the company had instant access to the company's most essential data and results — on their desktop PCs as well as their Blackberries.

What's most important to note: "This wasn't just an IT-feat," Seral says. "It was about changing the culture so everyone has a common way to look at the business."[1] The wowie-zowie nature of digital dashboards is not the real story. Technological possibilities are merely pushing new questions to the front of the debate: How much information do we really want to share with everyone? Are we willing and able to create a culture where we trust more people with more information, so they can manage more of their own decisions? The largest hurdle companies will face in creating more transparent decision-making tools is cultural, not technological.

What's important to note next: The more information people have that's useful and helpful in making daily decisions, the more they can see how their work affects the whole, and the more everyone has a sense of ownership. GE has built these dashboards for about one out of every 1,000 employees. That means 0.1% of their workforce has access to this decision-making tool. Still very hierarchical! If companies want transparency to be a competitive advantage, digital dashboards will have to reach much farther into organizations — down to most mid-managers. (Obviously, with data focused on their mid-level needs.) Steps 5–10 will give you the confidence to do so.

5

Loosen your controls, then study the trends and patterns

Overwhelmed by the complexities of today's marketplace, leading retailers are essentially letting vendors run much of their business. For example, Borders bookstores used to stock more than ten titles about sushi on their bookshelves. Now, they've cut that number in half. Why? Because HarperCollins, the nation's third largest publishing house, told them to. HarperCollins had better data and was closer to those stocking decisions than the bookseller.[2]

Why stop at vendors? If retailers can trust vendors to stock their shelves why can't you trust your mid-managers and employees with more supply chain decisions, resourcing decisions, and more? You can!

Loosening controls can pay off. According to Getthere.com, about 52% of business travelers who have the option of booking online —

and bypassing corporate travel departments — are doing so. And the trend is growing. Travel site Expedia says that one big company confided that Expedia was showing up as the number one charge on corporate cards, despite the fact that employees weren't supposed to be using it at all.[3] More companies are reversing themselves, allowing employees to book travel arrangements on their own, as the costs of controlling travel costs (maintaining a travel department and enforcing its rules) are becoming more costly than letting people do it themselves.

Why is this so important? The complexities *inside* your company are no different from those in the marketplace. You need to turn over more day-to-day decisions to the people who are closest to the problems — *without* losing control of costs and returns on investments.

Do so by building mid-manager tools that let you keep track of how good — or bad — those decisions are....

Consider this: In 2003, a brilliant computer scientist at the University of Washington named Oren Etzoioni announced that he had succeeded in deriving patterns in airplane seat pricing over time. Etzoioni claims his new software can tell you whether you should book now, wait until Sunday night, or hold off a couple weeks. If true, this could save corporations hundreds of millions of dollars a year. When told about it, one airline spokesperson said, "There are no patterns. We've looked, and there aren't any."[4] How employees make decisions (or anyone besides you, for that matter) may seem random and perplexing, but as the airline industry is now learning, all complex systems have patterns and trends. You just need to know where to look. The patterns are there, in your organization. You will soon be able to watch how mid-level and frontline employees make decisions, if...if you're willing to trust those decisions in the first place.

We are on the cusp of all this being very real. "We're discovering the 'physics' of business," says Irving Wladawsky-Berger, who runs IBM's On Demand business unit, which sells IT access to customers when they need it. "It's sort of like trying to unravel the business genome. We're asking our researchers — mathematicians, computer scientists and systems experts, and even anthropologists and sociologists — to look at business processes and decision-making in a much more systematic and serious way."[5]

Examples of transparency are popping up everywhere, and can be used to your advantage. Verizon CIO Shaygan Kheradpir used to negotiate discounts with each of the firm's computer vendors. A time-consuming approach, and not the best use of his talents. So Kheradpir loosened controls in the negotiating process, and has his staff research whatever they want to buy on eBay. With defunct dot-coms selling their wares, "it's as if you now have a stock market for servers," says Kheradpir. While Verizon's procedures prevent him from buying on eBay — (he's trying to change that) — he's better informed about pricing, and uses what he's learned to negotiate better deals, more quickly. All based on trends he found in transparent information.[6]

Reinvent...

6

Performance Management and

7

Training and Development

to reflect the new approach to open information sharing. Teach people how better to manage themselves and their own performance.

(See next chapters for more)

8

...and how the financial folks focus on human capital

There are clear signs that finance teams are squaring up for a turf war with human resource people. According to a 2003 report by CFO Resource Services, *Human Capital Management — The CFO's Perspective*, finance execs expect to have significantly more influence over the HR function within the next two years. Up until now, employees have been seen as costs. However, when viewed as human capital — which sees the training and development of employees as an investment that can produce measurable returns — finance-types believe they can get a lot more out of that investment. There is still a way to go. The report states that companies spend, on average, 36% of their revenue on employees, yet only 16% of the financial officers have more than a moderate understanding of their labor costs.[7] Why is this step so important? Because steps 4–10 advocate much greater openness in sharing of information than most execs are used to. To mitigate the potential risks, execs will need new and more robust data on their labor costs and investments, and how employees use the information they will be sharing.

9

Track the success of increased transparency by studying how much employees trust your systems to help them succeed and

10

Factor in how much those systems reinforce the values, principles, and ideals of the organization

Ultimately, transparency is about trust. And values. The more you trust your employees, the more information you'll give them to manage both their success and the company's success. And the more trust you exhibit, the more you live your core values.

•

Most every generation has had access to more information than their parents did. Yet, Gen Y (those born after 1980) has grown up with Net-like expectations for access and transparency. How will you attract and retain this generation? How transparent can you be for them? How you address this question will be a critical component in the war for their talent for many years to come. And every Gen Y employee's ability to trust in the company's leadership, tools, processes, goals, and mission will be affected by your degree of transparency.

WANT MORE?

- *Beyond Branding: How the New Values of Transparency and Integrity Are Changing the World of Brands,* edited by Nicholas Ind
  The fourteen authors believe that "transparency…opens a bigger opportunity to the natural dance of human desire and energy than tightly constructed strategies that are policed, with lock-step practices, laminated mission statements and all the rest…"
- http://www.valuetrue.com
- http://www.transparency.org

30
How to
Fix Performance Management

WHY IT NEEDS FIXING

Even though human behavior is one of the most complex things on the planet, most companies try to manage it simplistically — using carrots and sticks to get people to do what they want them to. There's got to be a better way. A more robust way, that matches people's very human need to manage themselves.

Ten Essentials for Simpler Companies

Don't aim to manage more or manage better.
Build better tools, training, and support for employees so they can better manage themselves

THE CLASSICS

Always been important…and becoming more so

❶

Have clear goals

❷

Make sure managers and employees contract with each other about meeting those goals

3

Train managers to meet those goals with ongoing conversations, check-ins, and evaluations with employees

THE NEW ESSENTIALS

Developing new ways to help every individual manage his or her own performance.

4

Improve how everyone has valuable conversations

Some managers are really good at using day-to-day conversations to coach, mentor, praise, and evaluate. Most are not. The success of any performance management system is based on a manager's ability to have meaningful and useful conversations with each person they supervise.

5

Enrich and broaden your coaching and mentoring efforts

Business has embraced a really good thing — we all need coaches and guides. Don't stop there! No matter how successful your current coaching and mentoring efforts are, take whatever you're doing and double it. In Corning's R&D labs, for example, scientists get two coaches — one is assigned the role of "motivator," and another acts as the "bridge," making cross-functional connections between the scientist and other people in the organization. Both coaches are held accountable for both the scientist's success and the department's success. This is one way of making certain that every scientist at Corning finds ways to use all of their talents, and is given the chance to be a top performer.

6

Drive cultural change among your senior team

Help them see the business case for looking beyond organizational productivity, into more personal views of performance…

Jumping the Chasm

FROM ONLY...	TO INCLUDE...
Organizational productivity: Managing to get more out of less resources	**Personal productivity:** Making it possible for each individual to accomplish more
Operational excellence: Managing every process and outcome to ensure continuous improvement	**Radical simplicity:** Focusing on what people need to do their best
Operational consolidation: Eliminating duplication and waste, using scale to get more done with less resources	**Business units of one:** Use technology and information transparency to identify the needs of each individual
Business sophistication pushed down	**Work sophistication pushed up:** The people on the front lines know as much about work as you know about business. We need to move beyond suggestion programs to truly *learning from* our workforce

7

Innovate:

Change the way you think about company tools and processes

Jill Smith works from home watching over her four kids, not in her own business, but doing work that most companies would force her into a call center to do. She works as a reservation agent for JetBlue airlines. And Jill isn't a special case. JetBlue's entire force of 550 agents work out of their own homes. CEO David Neeleman says the company saves 20% on booking costs by doing it this way instead of through call centers, and has kept staff turnover rate extremely low.[1] This is your future. Sci-fi author William Gibson has famously said, "the future has already arrived. It's just not evenly distributed yet." Technology and information transparency are making it possible to completely reshape corporate processes into personal processes. For example, Cisco formed its Workplace Resources Unit to respond to employee productivity needs. In Silicon Valley and elsewhere, they created way-stations, located half-way between where most of their employees lived and the company's main campuses. More than one third of their workforce now make regular use of mobile workplace options. Changes like this go well beyond mere mobility of work. It's an attitude, a belief, it's a cultural thing. If people are going to be asked to be more productive, leaders must be willing to design more around those people's needs.

(For more on this trend — My Work My Way — see *Work 2.0*)

8

Ensure that all performance management tools and processes are two-way:

Performance management, as practiced in most companies, is still mostly a one-way system. Companies like Kraft and Hewlett-Packard now use a Web-based time-sheet manager that includes software to display two productivity barometers on each employee's PC. One measures that person's productivity, the other measures their team's — each tracks performance against a pre-determined bonus target.[2] But did every employee sign up to meet that target? Do they have all the tools and support they need to meet it? Are the deadlines and goals realistic? Is their manager helpful, or a pain in the butt? Although there is no argument that these factors affect productivity, all that's figured into the barometers are tasks completed within certain timeframes. If companies are truly interested in getting the best out of everyone, they must provide real-time, in-depth, two-way evaluations, where employees can tell companies what they need to do their best.

9

Tie improved training and development to improved performance management

To keep improving their performance, employees need to keep learning. Treat training and development and performance management as inseparable. (For more, see next chapter, Step 8)

10

Communicate, communicate, communicate...

This approach to performance management is different in many ways from current practices. And, like any change, its success will depend on how well everyone understands, and is engaged in the changes.

From: Performance management now asks every individual to take a holistic view of a company's needs and its view of success, and act accordingly.

To: This approach introduces a mirror image, in which the focus is on each individual's needs, the company takes a holistic view of each individual. The new criteria are:

- Know me
- Know my work
- Know what I need
- Know how to help me

Once, the only way this could happen was person to person — with the burden solely on the immediate supervisor. Now, technology and information transparency makes it possible in many more ways. The only question that remains: Do we have the *will and desire* to know our employees well enough to build better tools, training, and support for them, so they can better manage themselves?

31

How to Fix Training and Development

WHY IT NEEDS FIXING

Training can occur without learning and without deep development, but that's expensive for both the company and the individual. And right now, that's what's happening a lot of the time.

Ten Essentials for Simpler Companies

Find cheaper, more powerful ways to help people learn more, and more quickly

THE CLASSICS

Always been important…and becoming more so

Seven Principles of Learning

Source: Adapted from Institute for Research on Learning

❶

Learning is fundamentally social

The more you invest in mentoring, coaching, and collaboration tools, the more people can teach each other — with little or no additional budget allocations.

❷

Learning is embedded in communities, groups, and teams

The more you invest in collaboration tools and processes, the more workteams and communities of practice can teach each other.

❸

Learning is an act of participation

The more you can get people out of classrooms or online forums, and have them trying and applying stuff, the faster they'll learn and the more they'll retain what they learn. Action learning is the way to go! Training and development *must* be just-in-time (or as close to that as possible) and *immediately* applicable on the job.

❹

Knowing is a part of, but different from learning. Knowing depends on engagement

People will learn morebetterfaster if you engage their hearts, if you ignite their passions, if you awaken them to new possibilities. The more you do, the cheaper training and development becomes — because it can be done less often, with better results.

❺

Engagement is inseparable from empowerment

Let people try, fail, be coached, and try again. The more restrictive and regimented and compliance-driven training and development is, the slower its uptake, the slower its application, the slower you'll see bottom-line impact.

❻

Failure to participate results in failure to learn

When communication is one-way, and you restrict pushback from below…learning slows down, and very little of it sticks. Which means you have to be directive, repeating those directives over and over again with each new change.

7

People are natural life-long learners (as long as they're not bored)

Remember kindergarten? Every minute was alive with something new to learn! People are hard-wired to be intensely curious and learn something new just about every moment of their life. Then along comes corporate training and development with learning objectives, agendas, and handouts….Zzzzzzzzzzzzzzzzzz. Surprise and excite people, and they learn morebetterfaster. Amaze, incite, provoke, tease, stimulate, challenge, and immerse people, and they learn morebetterfaster. Touch their emotions — joy, sadness, celebration, love, fear, frustration, caring, tenderness — and they'll carry with them what they learned wherever they go. The more your formal training and development experiences embed the true joy and wonder of learning, employees will bring their entire selves to every session.

THE NEW ESSENTIALS

Connecting learning to real-world, get-it-done-now, demands and responsibilities

8

Tie improved performance management to improved training and development

"Connect the dots" between information transparency, performance management, and training and development:

- Departmental digital dashboards could indicate specific areas where team training and development is necessary
- Build new worktools that create a seamless flow between managing daily tasks and getting just-in-time training

- Build two-way feedback loops into performance management tools to ensure constant bottom-up feedback on managers, shaping their own training and development
- If you track Clarity/Navigation/Fulfillment/Usability/Speed/ and Time, you will likely find that many of your training and development needs are *actually* problems with your tools, infrastructure, content, process, or delivery

  All of which may be less costly to fix than more investments in training.

9

We live in the attention economy.

Deal with it. Now.

You have seconds, not hours or days.

And it's only gonna get worse

Among the most precious assets people have to invest every day are their time and attention. Your training and development programs must respect those limited assets and pack the most value into the smallest space. Here's a sampling of ways to do that:

Layer content: People should be able to access the 15-second version of a training module and then decide if they need or want the 5-minute version, or the 15-minute version, etc. (Forcing people into "all or nothing at all" versions does not acknowledge how much control they have over their attention, and therefore fails to deliver full value.)

Be sure that every program answers these five questions immediately (no more than 10% to 20% into the content):

- How is this relevant to my current job and responsibilities?
- What are the immediate next steps after this training?
- What does successful application of this training look like?
- What follow-up tools and support do I get after this session is over?
- WIIFM, What's in it for me? (How do I, personally, benefit from this training?)

You may wish to hold off on answering some of these questions until you're deeper into the material. Don't! Because no more than 20% into your program, your learners' minds are drifting off to these questions. Grab their attention before they drift!

Follow the Grand Poobah Law: If you can't get it on one page, you haven't yet gotten to the essence of what you want people to learn.

Understand who your competition is: MTV, Disney, Nickelodeon, interactive science museums, the entire Internet, and more.... You don't own the right to use your employee's time and attention. Every day you must *compete* for it. And every day, your people are bombarded with infotainment, edutainment, and technotainment. Recognize that they have been trained to listen and pay attention in ways that might not fit what you were planning.

Design five-minute chunks: No matter how long the training is overall, think in terms of five-minute modules

Design follow-up dialogues: People love to talk to each other. After training events, you create more value by suggesting questions and conversations that will help them use what they've learned

Design follow-up content, tease them with it: Like marketers who keep prospects coming back for more, trainers need to keep people curious and engaged

Interactivity and hands-on experimentation work better than case studies

Stories work better than detailed explanations

Pictures, graphics, video, and sound work better than words

Just-in-time training and development is most valuable to most people

⑩

Manage the attention economy paradox:

Create the space and time to think, debate, challenge, probe, question, provoke, and make connections

As we try to move more things off our to-do lists every day, hardly anyone has enough time to reflect and think deeply. We rely on training and development to make that time available to us. Here's the paradox: While people *do* need one-page checklists and quick answers to five key questions, they *also* need completely open space, without regimented agendas in which they can make connections between ideas, information, and people. The challenge for training and development is to create a balance between the need for tightly structured use of time and attention, and unstructured opportunities for people to grow and make their own connections.

32

How to
Spot Tomorrow's Great Places to Work

Great workplaces will do right by you, focus on your well-being, trust you, and invest in you and your teammates. But tomorrow's great places to work will also focus on your work —and help you accomplish morebetterfaster in an increasingly complex world.

Ten Essentials for Simpler Companies

Master today's best practices, and invent tomorrow's

THE CLASSICS

Always been important...and becoming more so

All great workplaces focus on...

(Based upon criteria from the Great Place to Work Institute)

❶

Credibility

- Communication is open and accessible
- The company builds great teams, organizes resources, and gets employees the materials and resources they need to do their work
- The company promotes its vision with consistency and integrity

2

Respect

- Professional development is supported and appreciated
- The company collaborates with employees and managers on relevant decisions
- The company demonstrates care and understanding for employees' personal lives, diverse backgrounds, and experiences

3

Fairness

- Equity: compensation, benefits, rewards, and recognition are balanced, fair, and appropriate
- Impartiality: there is no favoritism in hiring, advancement, or access to opportunities
- Justice: Discrimination is prohibited and there is a process in place for appeals

4

Pride

- Employees feel pride in their personal contribution and their ability to make a difference
- They take pride in the work produced by their team
- And they are proud of the company's products and standing in the community

5

Camaraderie

- Individuals feel accepted for who they are
- The company is socially welcoming, friendly, and even fun
- There is a shared sense of family among employees

•

Some Variations of Classic Essentials

The Gallup organization tests for employee satisfaction. It asks employees to agree or disagree with the following:[1]

- I know what is expected of me at work
- I have the materials and equipment I need to do my work
- I have the opportunity to do what I do best every day
- In the past week, I have been praised for doing good work
- My supervisor or someone else at work seems to care about me as a person
- Someone at work encourages my development
- My opinions seem to count
- My company's mission makes me feel my job is important
- I have a best friend at work
- In the past six months, someone at work has talked to me about my progress
- In the past year, I have had opportunities to learn and grow at work

•

Consulting firm Career Innovation uses an Inspiration at Work survey to track both personal fulfillment and corporate success

- Impact and Contribution: The ability to make a personal and meaningful impact through your organization
- Innovation and Growth: Your readiness for innovation and learning
- Trust and Relationships: The quality of your interaction with people who can support your career

THE NEW ESSENTIALS

Tomorrow's great places to work will pay a lot more attention to *what it takes to do great work*. They will recognize that it's no longer acceptable to say that there's *work* and there's *life* and it's up to employees to balance the two. They'll recognize that better workplaces must be designed with an eye to how work impacts the quality of our lives.

6
Return on, and respect for, employee assets

It doesn't matter that standard accounting practices ignore the plain truth: that companies use employee assets — time, attention, ideas, knowledge, passion, energy, and social networks — to make their company go. These assets are owned by the employees and can only be given freely, and voluntarily. Employees are beginning to think about how well or poorly companies use their contributions. They're beginning to ask: "Why should we invest these assets in you? If an hour, or day, or month, or year invested in your firm could be invested with a competitor, who would provide the better return?" Tomorrow's great places to work will treat employees as investors, whether they show up on the books that way or not.

(For more, see Chapters 25–31, and *Work 2.0*)

7
Willingness and ability to embrace transparency

The amount of transparency around us (the free-flow of information from any source, anywhere in the world) is increasing at an incredible rate. We are crossing a threshold where the barriers to total transparency — technology, content, access, costs — continue to fall. It is becoming, or soon will be, physically possible for every employee in every company to easily access all customer data and trends, all corporate performance data and trends, all personal performance evaluations and trends, all collaboration trends and content, all strategic plan content, all project content, all process content, all inventory data and trends (and on, and on)...that the company chooses to make available for frontline and mid-level decision-making. **There's the rub!** The usual barriers, such as costs and technological capability, are falling at a much faster rate than most corporate cultures have changed. Tomorrow's great places to work will embrace transparency as an opportunity for competitive advantages. They will drive more complete transparency closer to the frontlines than their competitors.

(For more, see Chapters 25–31, and *Work 2.0*)

8

Ability to deliver personal productivity

Once companies embrace greater transparency, completely new possibilities open up. Right now, most companies focus only on organizational productivity because that's the data that's collected and shared with top dog decision-makers. But with more fluid sharing of team data, customer data, 360° degree feedback, and much more, frontline decision-makers can focus more effectively on their own performance — without having to wait for a manager or company evaluation.

•

We have a workforce who is ready, willing, and able to produce far more than any leader can imagine! Tomorrow's great places will tap into that potential by focusing on personal productivity. The new criteria, no longer left solely to one's manager, are:

- Know me
- Know my work
- Know what I need
- Know how to help me

Tomorrow's great places to work will do more to get each individual what they need to do their best and produce the greatest output with the least effort.

(For more, see Chapters 25–31, and *Work 2.0*)

9

Great workplaces are great, yet...

It's the work, baby... It's the work!

And it's peer-to-peer value

Jensen Group research and IBM Extreme Blue (IBM's summer internship program to attract the best of the best MBAs and technologists)[2] independently came to the same conclusion: It's the work, baby! For top talent everywhere, of all ages, but especially among Generation Y (born after 1980), here's what we found counts the most in attracting and keeping that talent:

1. **Great Projects**

   The top priority: "Is the work that I'm doing really important? Is it truly going to make a difference or change the world?"

2. **Great People**

   The same as, yet more impatient than, all that we've heard before. The battle cry among the talent you most want to keep, "Lose all the loser managers! Surround me with only the best of the best, or lose me."

3. **Great Place to Work**

   Universal basics: trust, fairness, accountability, clear goals, great leadership, fair pay, great communication, lots of recognition, etc.

4. **Wow Experiences**

   "Is my work portfolio filled with great experiences? Can the organization help me enrich my portfolio of experiences?"

Notice the nuances: The usual criteria for great places to work *are* important! But they've dropped to third place. First and second are the work itself and the people surrounding the employee — are both insanely great? Not just most-of-the-time good, but killer great? And when there are the occasional speed bumps, where we all must do some less-than-great work, is the company focused on helping to build a portfolio of *experiences* — not just career moves or jobs.

•

There's another theme that requires leadership's utmost attention: the creation of peer-to-peer value. Boasting of an open, sharing, and collaborative environment nowadays is like saying, "We're a great place to work. We provide air for our employees to breathe! Flushable toilets too!"

•

Years ago, people needed companies around them to facilitate and enhance their collaboration. We couldn't do it without those entities. Now, nobody needs companies anymore just to help them collaborate, share, or create. People can now self-organize amazingly well, thank you. Technology and the current free-flow of information is making tons of collaboration beyond corporate walls not only possible, but often desirable. The real challenge for everyone — where we do need corporate resources, structure, and skills — is getting the most out of each connection, often in the least amount of time. That's peer-to-peer value. But true value is only present if companies design collaborative environments that are as user-centered as they are corporate-driven.

•

The future of collaboration in great places to work will be tracking how much value it provides to each individual, as compared to the value they could find in any other free-market collaborative space, outside of the company. People will be attracted by and stay wherever they get the most value.

(For more, see *Work 2.0*)

10

Willingness and ability to address the last taboo.

It's not sex. It's not drinking, It's stress – and it's soaring*

Most companies have done a fairly poor job of making morebetterfaster manageable for the people who do the work. And that ineffectiveness is showing up in ways that few are measuring. It's a dirty little secret hidden out in the open. And it's having an impact on the bottom line.

* Thank you, *Fortune* magazine for such a wonderful headline! It's yours, I'm just borrowing it.[3]

Do-Less

Toolkit

One-page, tear-out summaries

of the key tools and ideas

that will help you

do less

and accomplish more

Three Laws of Workplace Behavior

❶

Ease-of-use and reduced-use-of-time
are equal to — and sometimes more important than —
recognition, compassion, inclusion, rewards,
penalties, loyalty, and hierarchy
in their ability to drive human behaviors.

❷

The Number One behavior in business today is
moving to-do's onto someone else's plate.

In most cases, this isn't mean-spirited or malingering.
It's merely an effective way of coping with too many to-do's,
too little time, and too few resources

❸

Once begun, work follows the path of least resistance.

Most of us manage our daily workload through triage:
We avoid or postpone all but the most pressing decisions and tasks.
And when everybody is in triage mode, the path of least resistance is to just keep things moving, passing work on to others as quickly as possible, even if that work comes up short in focus or importance. Because the biggest wall of resistance comes from stopping the flow and telling our bosses what they want us to do isn't focused, important, or valid.

See back for more

Three Laws•O•Less

Corresponding with the three laws of workplace behavior on reverse side

❶	So What? for execs	So What? for everyone
Make it easier for people to do things your way, and you'll get your way more often.	If you are user-centered — working backwards from the needs of your employees — you can drive as much change, compliance, and commitment as you currently get with traditional, top-down leadership tools and controls. (If not more!)	Treat people's time and attention as precious, and more people will do what you ask of them more often

❷	So What? for execs	So What? for everyone
It's fairly easy to get you to do someone else's to-do's, unless you learn how to push back.	(If this is what you want…) There is almost no limit to how much moremoremore you can squeeze out of people, as long as you suppress pushback from below. The universal behavior of pushing work onto someone else's plate will always keep things moving for you	Learn to push back (in ways that don't create defensiveness.) Or become a permanent victim of downhill to-do's. It's that brutally simple

❸	So What? for execs	So What? for everyone
It's a lot easier than you think to reduce the flow of work from your boss	Never push work back onto his/her plate. Always clarify immediate, short-term next steps. Clarification is your focusing, reducing tool	Never push work back onto his/her plate. Always clarify immediate, short-term next steps. Clarification is your focusing, reducing tool

Ten Simple Truths

about doing less and accomplishing more

1

Simplicity is about power

(The power to do less of what *doesn't matter* and more of *what does*)

Which means, like all sources of power throughout human history,

it brings out the best and worst in people

2

Simplicity in the workplace is the disciplined practice of empathy and common sense

It is based on human nature and common sense, not corporate logic

It is the practice of working backwards from the needs of those doing the work

3

There are three basic reasons for doing less at work...

- "Work is important, but it is not life. I want to focus on all that life outside of work has to offer."
- "I want to make a difference. The work I do must matter.
  So I focus only on what I believe matters."
- "I want to be the best I can be. So I focus on what excites me and helps me grow."

Which means:

- Doing less and laziness are not the same thing
- Each individual must decide why s/he wants to do less, and live every day according to that decision

4

In most of today's workplaces:

Work = Figuring out what to do with finite time and attention, and infinite information and choices

5

You have a lot more control over your workload than you think you do

It comes down to where and how you choose to focus your time and attention.

No one but you controls those things

continued on bac

Ten Simple Truths

about doing less and accomplishing more

6

It is no longer acceptable to say that there's *work* and there's *life* and it's up to employees to balance the two

Everything an employer does and asks of you uses a portion of your life

7

To build better workplaces,
we must first see how the design of work impacts the quality of our lives

Employers ask you to invest your assets — time, attention, ideas, knowledge, passion, energy, and social networks — to make their companies go. We all must examine how well, or poorly, companies use our assets

8

R-E-S-P-E-C-T now includes how well, or poorly, your company, your manager, and your teammates use the finite time you have available every day

(And how well, or poorly, you use theirs!)

9

We live in the Attention Economy:
Every project is about bartering for someone's time and attention

Employees may tolerate management's logic, but act on their own conclusions of what deserves their time and attention

10

Plan and manage and change all you want.
Just know that execution travels at the speed of sense-making

Create less clutter and more clarity, or help everyone make sense of it faster than the competition, and you win

The Most Important Number in Business No One Ever Talks About

1440

1440 is the number of minutes in a day.

No one can change that. There is no Executive Suite to which you can appeal for more minutes in your daily budget. There is no way to accrue minutes for tomorrow's daily budget.
The end of the day is just that. Done. *Kaput*. No do overs.

So What? for execs

It could be time to wake up and smell the coffee. You can plan, budget, manage, and change. And you can strategize, operationalize, harmonize, synergize, rationalize, penalize, reward, compensate, motivate, and (insert your buzzwords-of-choice here) all that you want.
But at the end of the day (literally), a lot of human behavior is driven by time- and attention-squeezes. At least equally as much as any leadership lever you pull.
Work = Figuring out what to do with finite time and attention, and infinite information and choices. More people in your organization than ever before are making daily choices based not on what's in the plan, or what they're rewarded to do or penalized not to do,
or even what they're passionate about — but based on whatever they can squeeze into a finite number of minutes. The more morebetterfaster you push onto each individual's day, the more
the clock, and not your plan, will influence their decisions.
The way out. Work backwards from people's needs. Study how you use their time and attention, *from their perspective, not yours!* Improve that, and the possibilities are limitless!

So What? for everyone

Daily choices, decisions, and actions. It comes down to where and how you choose to focus your time and attention. Now matter what the economy does, or your boss does, or how the company wants you to cut costs — no one but you controls how your time and attention are spent. If you choose not to believe that, think about this: the next time you spend an extra five minutes on that email, or in that meeting, or on that phone call, you are stealing five minutes from your kid, or your spouse, or yourself. Since there are only 1440 minutes and never more, whatever you give to The Man must come from somewhere else.
Career and life planning. Your time is just one asset that you own. The others include your attention, ideas, knowledge, passion, energy, and your social networks. Your bosses and customers want you to invest these things in them. As you make career and life choices, you must do so by examining how well, or poorly, your company and customers are using these assets.
And whether or not you should go elsewhere for a better return.

Three Tools for
Cutting Through Clutter and Competing on Clarity

Can be used in both listening/probing/questioning, as well as clarifying/communicating/sharing

❶

Know, Feel, Do

KNOW "What's the one thing I want people to know, understand, learn, or question?"
Your answer should be no longer than one sentence. Write it down. Rehearse it.

FEEL "How do I want people to feel when I'm done?"
Your answer should be no longer than one sentence. Write it down. Rehearse it.

DO "What do I want people to do as a direct result of my communication?"
Your answer should be no longer than one sentence. Write it down. Rehearse it.

❷

Behavioral Communication

This is the anatomy of a decision
When people choose between being compliant, acting with full commitment, or doing nothing at all, these are the five questions they think about, and want answered

How is this relevant to what I do?

What, specifically, should I do?

What do success and failure look like?

What tools and support are available?

WIIFM — What's in it for me?

❸

CLEAR Communication

These are the answers to each behavioral question. If you wish to compete on clarity, and speed up implementation, you must provide this information, or create ways for people to figure it out themselves

Connection to their workload

List action steps

Expectations for success

Ability to achieve success

Return to that person

See back for applying these tools to emails, voicemails, meetings, presentations

For more:
The Simplicity Survival Handbook

How to delete 75% of your emails Chapter 2

1. If BOTH the Subject and the Sender fail to create this reaction:
I have to read or at least scan this today.
DO NOT open or scan the message. Hit Delete immediately

2. Scan the remaining messages for two bits of information:
• Action you must take • Date or deadline for that action, within the next 2 to 3 weeks
If the messages do not contain an action and a short-term date, delete them.

How to quickly prepare for any communication Chapter 3

1–3. Use: Know, Feel, Do
Write down one sentence for each. Time commitment: from 15 secs to 5 mins

---

How to leave shorter voicemails for better results Chapter 4

1–3. Use: Know, Feel, Do
Cover each of the three points in your message. Time of message: Never more than 30 secs

---

How to write shorter emails for better results Chapter 5

1–5. Use: CLEAR
Nail each of the five points in the CLEAR tool within top 3"x5"
Always remember that you are writing a billboard, not a letter. You must grab their attention!

How to do less and still deliver an awesome presentation Chapter 6

1. (Based on Know, Feel, Do...) Turn the one thing you want people to Know into a question
Engaging participants in a dialogue on that point will use up one-third to half your allotted time

2. Have a one-page summary that spells out, from *their* perspective: What This Means to You

---

How to go to fewer meetings and get more out of them Chapter 7

1. Remember one number: 1440 (number of minutes in a day)
It should inform most every choice you make about most every meeting you attend

2. Ask yourself how much value you'll *get* from this meeting — your ROI. You deserve bigger ROI's!

3. Ask yourself how much value you'll *contribute* — don't go if others can contribute more

Anatomy of a Great One-Hour Numbers-Driven Presentation

- *Every* presentation should always be about creating great dialogue, not 'presenting'
- *Never* more than ten pages

PAGE	TALKING POINTS	TIME
1 **Title Page:** "See, I'm using your jargon. I'm packaging my work by using Senior Exec phrases and themes-of-the-month."	• Be absolutely clear about the purpose of meeting, the reason for this presentation, and what you'll be asking for when you're done	**30 secs**
2 **"Here's everything I have to tell you, on just one page."**	• 5-6 bullet points providing an overview of your entire presentation. All but one of these points portray a reality the exec wants to see: Things are on-budget, on-time, etc. • Don't deliver spreadsheets — tell a story! Use headlines! Are you on top of things? That's what execs quickly want to know: What in your presentation will reassure them, or increase their risk-exposure when they have to present to *their* bosses? (For example: "We're On Target! $50 MM") • 1 bullet point should present a problem you want the exec to address. (If you've demonstrated that most of your presentation is about being a good soldier, and you're only presenting one challenge out of 5–6 points, they'll gladly help you problem-solve this one point.) • If you are successful, most of your time should be spent on this one page	**15 – 30 mins** **You presenting:** 5 mins **Balance of time:** Execs questioning, debating, understanding what you're presenting

Great One-Hour Numbers-Driven Presentation

PAGE	TALKING POINTS	TIME
3 – 9 **The numbers and details behind your one-pager**	• Offer all the numbers — pie-charts, Excel spreadsheets, etc. — behind your one-pager. • Especially given all the recent accounting scandals, you must provide excruciatingly detailed numbers to have credibility. But spreadsheets and data dumps should NEVER be the focus of your presentation. If you get sucked into a numbers-driven presentation, you've just increased your workload, while reducing the executive's. Is that how you want to work?	**10 – 15 mins**
10 **"Here's what we need from you, so we can succeed."**	• 3–5 bullet points providing an overview of what you need from the senior exec. Be as specific as you can (See Step 6) • This page is supercritical. If you don't focus on this, every presentation will be made in corporate purgatory: constantly making presentations, but getting nothing out of them in return	**5 – 10 mins** **You presenting:** 2 – 5 mins **Balance of time:** Engaging senior execs in their role in your project

A Mini-Course in Saying "No"

❶ First, recognize that there are two different kinds of "no's"

Direct — "No." • "No. Thank you, though." • "Too busy. I'll pass."

With Whom
- Close teammates, friends, those who know how often you say yes
- People with whom you have little or no personal connection

How Often — About 25% of all opportunities to say no

Indirect — "Help me understand..." • "Let's talk about this..."

With Whom
- Bosses, customers, leaders: Those who direct your actions
- Networked teammates: Those in the same company, group, or team, but not tied to your daily routine

How Often — About 75% of all opportunities to say no

Important fact and strategy: While Direct No's account for only a quarter of your opportunities to push back, that's where most of us spend most of our time! Because these are comfortable no's, low-risk, almost-fun no's. Your goal is to spend as little time, emotion, and energy here as possible. Invest whatever you've saved into Indirect No's.

❷ Treat Indirect No's as an opportunity to change a <u>relationship</u>, to build mutual respect

DO NOT focus on getting rid of the work you've just been handed. That will only make things worse.
Instead, focus on how your response *this* time will create *future* expectations — yours and theirs.
Take the indirect approach to manage the *overall flow* of to-do's from these individuals

DO focus on the conversation.

Control what you can, and forget the rest.
You can change the exchange.
You can change how you react.

See back for more on changing the exchange

A Mini-Course in Saying "No"

Indirect No's: Focus on three things, always leading with questions...

- **Discover the Unsaid**

  Thanks for your confidence in me! Why'd you think of me?

  Help me understand what you're trying to achieve...

  Help me understand the connection to my quarterly goals...

  What's connected to this project that's driving the deadline?

  What would success look like for this project?

  Once I hand this back to you, what happens next?

  Even if they are minimal, what tools/support/resources are available?

  What's worked in the past?

  What do you wish you could have changed last time?

  What else is on your plate besides this project?

- **Explore Alternative Solutions**

  Ya know, Alpha Team had a problem like this...How about if we...?

  What if I presented two solutions that stayed within the budget?

  Here's how I'd start...What am I missing?

  Looking at what's already on my plate, what can I put on hold?

  Which of these three approaches do you think is best?

  Are there others who should be involved in this?

  Can I outsource this to a contractor/vendor/consultant?

  Could I set up a mid-point check-in with you?

- **Contract for the Next Conversation**

  I'll make it go away, Chief! Could we set up a debrief talk afterwards?

  To get this project done, others fell off my plate:
  Can you help me find a way to avoid that next time?

  I'd like to make suggestions to help do this even better next time, OK?

  I'm glad you're thrilled with how I delivered on this! —
  Now, can we talk about...?

If your goal is to reduce the overall flow of to-do's from someone, these three tracks of questions — **Discover, Explore, Contract** — work! Not necessarily by making any one task go away. But they deliver what you're really after: **Respect, Partnership**

What If My Boss Just Doesn't "Get It"?

If your boss truly doesn't get it, he or she *never* will.
So don't waste precious time, energy, and passions banging your head against a wall, trying to get this bozo to change.
Instead, conduct lots of conversations to confirm your own beliefs, and then use that information to make your next career move.

THREE WAYS TO DEAL WITH BOSSES WHO DON'T GET IT

❶ Smile and Nod

Speech bubble: "Sure boss, whatever you say."
Thought bubble: "I'll just keep doing it my way."

You've made a conscious decision to under-invest in the company because your repeated efforts to help make changes went unrewarded and unheeded. You recognize that this is a personal choice, and do not play the victim. No whining, back-stabbing, complaining, or gossiping about *them*. You invest energy, instead, in positive actions, like more time with family

❷ Go Around or Above

"I'd like to talk to you about a *business* decision, and some alternate approaches…"

You still believe in the company and its leadership, but see your immediate boss as a barrier to doing what's right. You never focus on the conflict with your boss. You're always focused on the merits of decisions made, and making the business case for new decisions

❸ Let Your Departure Do the Talking

Write Your Six-Months* Notice. But keep it at home.
Don't go public until you've found a new job.

You have determined that your boss is a barrier, and that the company is unwilling or unable to address the situation. Writing a Six Months Notice, while keeping it to yourself, is about being committed and being smart. (Set a goal for getting out, begin an active job search, but don't go public until it makes economic sense to do so.)

* The economy and market conditions may change the *timing*, but not the *outcome*.
No matter how long it takes, you have a proactive plan for getting out. In the meantime, you maintain a positive attitude and fulfill accountabilities at your current job.

How to Clarify Goals and Objectives More Quickly

It's usually not the goals themselves that are unclear.
What you're *supposed to do with them* is what's fuzzy — how the goals refocus or change your work.
To figure that out, you need to ask the five questions of Behavioral Communication...

Bottom line: Do not take on work until you understand what the goals mean to you, and the kind of work you should be doing.
That doesn't mean refusing work. It means pushing for clarity.

❶

As soon as your boss sets a new goal for you, or tells you about a new corporate objective, ask:
Help me understand how this changes what I've been doing?

❷

Then: **Got suggestions for my first steps? What's the best way to get started?**

❸

Then: **What does success look like?...**
What should I watch for to be sure I'm making progress, and am on target?

❹

Then: **What tools and support are available?**

❺

Finally: **WIIFM — What's in it for me? Or for us?**

You know to phrase this question properly, and with great care — right? Some approaches include, "Help me understand how this helps me achieve my goals?" and "How does this help our team be more successful?" Push for clarity here. All human beings, including you, are motivated, in part, by self-interest. It's OK to let that be part of your conversation. More than OK, it's required.

How to Get the Budget You Need and Deserve, with a Lot Less Effort

Most everything you've been told about how budgets are set is baloney.
If you jump through hoops to justify/quantify/rationalize/cut or supersize your numbers, you're playing with a stacked deck. (Stacked against you.)

❶

Do NOT focus on money

It's the very *last* thing you should discuss!

DO focus on the senior team's headaches.

Find out what's keeping the most senior members "awake at night."

(FUD is a biggie for many execs: Fear, Uncertainty, Doubt)

❷

Package your need for money to perfectly match the senior exec's very personal concerns

❸

Your first budget meeting with the Poobah should last no more than 15 minutes

Make your pitch, but also make a favorable impression. The shorter the better.

No handouts! Just you, and the key message.

What can you accomplish in 15 minutes or less? See Step 4.

❹

Closing your pitch:

DO NOT ask for money! Ask for another meeting

If you are invited back to a second meeting, you should have an 80% to 90% success rate in getting all or much of the budget you are requesting, because your Poobah helped initiate and shape the request

See back for more

How to Get the Budget You Need

The Budget-Setting Secret Hidden in Plain Sight

Why this four-step process works with 80% to 90% success rates...

Throughout human history in most of the world, **budget-setting has never been about money or strategy.** Setting budgets is about power, control, personalities, dreams, fantasies, revenge, pettiness, greed, caring, altruism, tithing, perception, sharing, fun, passion, vision, aspirations, discrimination, conflict, bartering, compromise, paybacks, payoffs, partnerships, and friendships — to name a few. Like work, budgets are personal. Even great business leaders with endless amounts of integrity, who truly follow their plans and strategies cannot rewrite the law that says budgets are, and always will be, personal. The people who get the most money know this.

Seven Rules for Working with Grand Poobahs

You know: senior execs…head honchos…big cheeses…corner office-dwellers

❶

Reduce everything to one page

Remember the Grand Poobah Law: If it has a staple in it, it doesn't get read.

Never walk into any meeting or presentation without a one-page summary (of display-size type) that spells out, from *their* perspective: What This Means to You

❷

Regardless of what the agenda says or the executive asked for…

Presentations* to senior executives are almost always going to be about one of two things:

- **Control**
- **Minimizing the executive's exposure to risk**

So, regardless of what you've been asked to present, and what details you're supposed to have covered, your story and your headline must always be:

- "Boss, things are under control / not under control."
- "Boss, whether my news is good or bad, your butt is safe with me."

* (*Presentation*, as opposed to an invitation for dialogue. That's very different.)

❸

Always shop your ideas around ahead of time

Typical senior execs hate two things: 1) Surprises. 2) Spending time on anything that their lieutenants haven't already vetted. Pre-selling your ideas to the lieutenants keeps you covered on both.

❹

The stated problem is never the problem

The perceived or stated problem is never the *whole* problem, and often not the *real* problem. Issues and challenges at the senior level are complicated, interconnected, and overlapping. You will have to dig deep.

continued on back

Seven Rules for Working with Grand Poobahs

❺

Data will set you free

(If it's used to tell a story or start a tough conversation)

Always use data to tell a story, NEVER to just present numbers and results.

Data can create uncomfortable discussions. That's good.

Be Switzerland: Detach from emotions and politics. Data are just facts and trends that leaders must figure out how to use. Present and facilitate from a neutral position

❻

Be a "pair of hands"

(Help with executive's day-to-day tasks and priorities, and be involved in delivering their messages and plans throughout the organization.)

Gets you in — behind those closed doors

❼

Always take the high road. Always!

Especially if alignment between senior team members breaks down, or politics grow: No matter how painful it gets, take the high road.

Tell the truth, take the blame, present bad news, whatever it takes.

Always be able to look at yourself in the mirror

RESPECT:
How to Change the Debate

Complete this survey, then flip to the back to see how to use it

SimplerWork Index™

Tracking the connections between great places to work and what it takes to do great work

	STRONGLY AGREE	AGREE	NEITHER AGREE / DISAGREE	DISAGREE	STRONGLY DISAGREE
1. Competing on Clarity My manager organizes and shares information in ways that help me work smarter and faster	○	○	○	○	○
2. Navigation In my workplace, it is easy for me to find whomever or whatever I need to work smart enough, fast enough	○	○	○	○	○
3. Fulfillment of Basics In my workplace, it is easy to get what I need to get my work done — right information, right way, right amount	○	○	○	○	○
4. Usability In my workplace, corporate-built stuff* is easy to use (*Tools, training, instructions, information technology, etc.; all that is designed to help you do your work)	○	○	○	○	○
5. Speed In my workplace, that same corporate-built stuff gets me what I need, as fast as I need it	○	○	○	○	○
6. Time My company is respectful of my time and attention, and is focused on using it wisely and effectively	○	○	○	○	○

continued on back

RESPECT: What needs to be new and different

All other views of respect in the workplace — decent pay, appropriate benefits, great culture, being treated fairly with open and honest communication, and much more — are still important! And always will be. But they're no longer enough. We need to expand our view of what it means to be treated respectfully.

Companies use your assets — time, attention, ideas, knowledge, passion, energy, and social networks — to make the profits they make. Yet, what kind of return are you getting for your assets: Is it getting easier to make a big impact at your company? How much of your time is spent doing great and important work? How much and how fast can you learn in your company? How challenging, rewarding, and exciting is your work? If you invested your assets in another employer, would you get a better return?

Respect goes beyond the soft stuff. It now must include how well, or poorly, your company, your manager, and your teammates use the assets you invest in them. (And how well, or poorly, you use theirs!) **This is all about personal productivity:** How much effort you have to put in to keep doing morebetterfaster. Respect in tomorrow's great workplaces will be about doing more to get each individual what they need to do their best and produce the greatest output with the least effort.

What you can do: Help change the debate

Unfortunately, business is only in the earliest stage of understanding and tracking personal productivity. Economic pressures and the war for talent will eventually force every company to focus on these dimensions, but you can't afford to wait that long! So…

1 Complete the survey

(go to www.simplerwork.com for an emailable version)

2 How do you feel?

Are you happy with how well your company scored? Most people are not. The favorable scores (Strongly Agree to Agree) are often as low as 12%, and usually top-off at about 50%. That's not good. Because the **six dimensions in the SimplerWork Index are six key *enablers*** — things that companies must do well, if they want you to continue to produce morebetterfaster.
(For more, see Chapter 26)

3 Take your feelings, opinions, and ideas public. Change the debate

The most constructive thing we can all do is to create a new kind of dialogue where respect for your time becomes as important to leaders as diversity, or safety, or working conditions, or global and generational differences, or career development paths. Because, while those things are now important to business leaders, they didn't start out that way. Most leaders weren't paying attention to those issues until the population at large started focusing on them. Personal productivity and how your time is used will become important when enough of us tell our leaders they're important.

Stay or Go Checklist

Delete more emails and run away from more meetings.
Stay if your manager and company support your efforts.
Go if they don't.

Set higher standards for information sharing and communication.
Push to get more of the information you need, the way you need it, in order to make fully-informed decisions.
Stay if your manager and company support your efforts.
Go if they don't.

Set higher standards for how you and your teammates organize and share what you know. And coach teammates who unknowingly pass on too much.
Stay connected with, and learn from, and laugh with teammates who get it.
Go elsewhere if they don't.

Change the way you interact with senior execs — one page summaries, helping them make better decisions, connecting with them as people and not as banks or strategists.
Stay if your leaders get it.
Go if they don't.

Learn how to say "no" in most any situation.
Stay if, more often than not, your decision is respected and enhances your career.
Go if it isn't and doesn't.

Learn how to question why you're getting the workload you're getting, and accept less of the party line and corporate spin.
Stay if, more often than not, your questions are answered truthfully and with integrity.
Go if they are not.

continued on back

Stay or Go Checklist

Learn how to deal with bosses who just don't get it, or who pile on too much.
Stay if your solutions work and are appreciated.
Go if they don't and aren't.

Learn how to research and ask tougher questions about how hard or easy your company makes it for you to do your best.
Stay if you like what you discover.
Go if you don't.

Learn how to track your own success in doing less, and continuously improve your do-less skills.
Stay if you're doing less, and that works for your company.
Go if you aren't and it doesn't.

Learn how to address the stupidity of some corporate structures, and help your company measure respect in completely new ways.
Stay if your leaders get it, and are trying.
Go if they don't and won't.

•

All that comes down to just one thing...
Really grasp how precious your daily 1440 minutes are.
And learn how to respect other people's 1440 minutes.
Stay if those around you also embrace this idea, helping you and others do their best.
Go if they don't.

Create Your Own Less•O•Meter

Instructions

1. Cut out needle
2. Push a fastener through **A** and **B**
3. Tack up on your wall
4. Move the needle according to what you're feeling the next time you're asked to do moremoremore, but your gut tells you that you should be doing lesslessless
5. If there's a difference between your current courage-state and what it needs to be to do less, call on your mentor, coach, buddies, or whip out your dog-eared copy of *Simplicity Survival Handbook*

Create Your Own Less•O•Meter

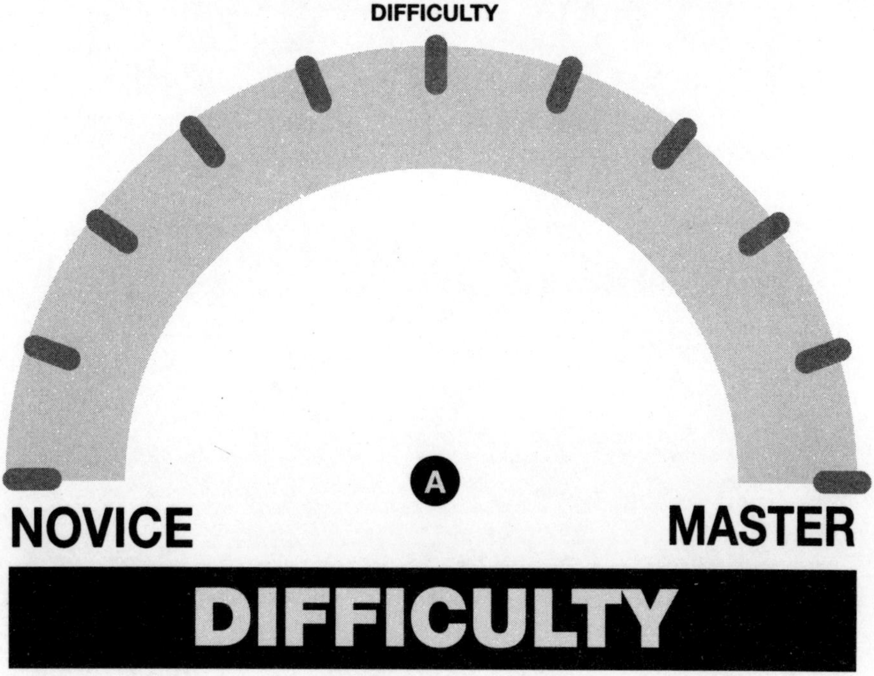

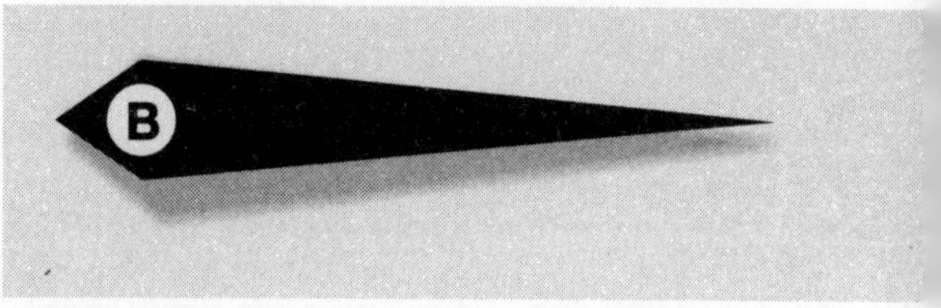

Instructions

1. Cut out needle
2. Push a fastener through **A** and **B**
3. Tack up on your wall
4. Move the needle according to what you're feeling the next time you're asked to do moremoremore, but your gut tells you that you should be doing lesslessless
5. If there's a difference between how easy it needs to be to do less and your current skill-level, call on your mentor, coach, buddies, or whip out your dog-eared copy of *Simplicity Survival Handbook*

Create Your Own Less•O•Meter

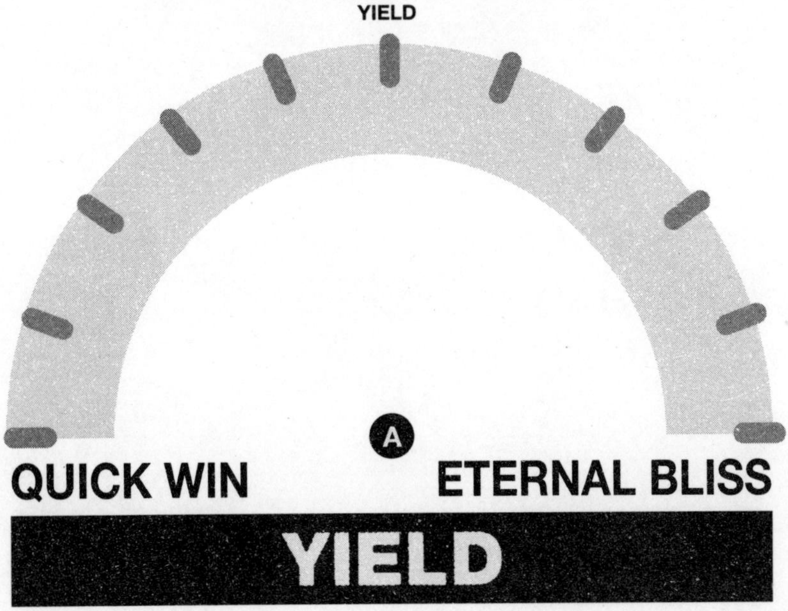

Instructions

1. Cut out needle
2. Push a fastener through **A** and **B**
3. Tack up on your wall
4. Move the needle according to what you're feeling the next time you're asked to do moremoremore, but your gut tells you that you should be doing lesslessless
5. If there's a difference between how much WIIFM you think you'll get from doing less and how much effort or angst it's gonna take, call on your mentor, coach, buddies, or whip out your dog-eared copy of *Simplicity Survival Handbook*

Endnotes

Chapter 2

1. The Jensen Group, ongoing research (1992-present), part of the study, *The Search for a Simpler Way*. These findings: Between 1998 and 2003, over 450 individuals who identified themselves as power users of email were asked, "How do you deal with email and connectivity overload?"
2. ibid.
3. ibid.
4. Jupiter Research, Email Marketing Report, October 16, 2001
5. ZDNet News, "Spam hist 36 percent of e-mail traffic," August 29, 2002
6. "Study Puts a Price on Spam," IDG News Service, July 2, 2003
7. See Footnote 1. In addition, these findings are based upon email questions asked of over 1,000 individuals between 1995 and 2003
8. Osterman Research, "Instant Messages Are Popping Up All Over," *Wall Street Journal*, June 12, 2003, page B4

Chapter 4

1. Based upon show-of-hands polls and written surveys taken during Jensen Group communication workshops between 1994 – 2003. Globally: several hundred thousand respondents.
2. ibid.
3. ibid.

Chapter 5

1. 1998 – 2003 Jensen Group ongoing user studies of over 1,000 people
2. ibid.

Chapter 6

1. "PowerPoint Goes to School," *Wall Street Journal*, November 13, 2002, B1
2. http://www.lisnews.com/article.php3?sid=20021113234907

Chapter 7

1. *Search for a Simpler Way*. These findings: While differences between workplaces precludes an accurate single list of Five Least Productive Activities, "How our team/company runs meetings" has consistently been among the top three to five
2. *Search for a Simpler Way*, over 400 respondents between 1999 and 2003
3. ibid., over 250 respondents between 1999 and 2003
4. *Work 2.0: Building The Future*, One Employee At A Time, by Bill Jensen, page 14

Chapter 9

1. "Dollars and Sense," *Red Herring*, October 2002, page 21
2. "New Atlanta Mayor Points a Way Out of City Fiscal Hole," *Wall Street Journal*, February 14, 2003, page 1
3. "Career Journal," *Wall Street Journal*, February 4, 2003, page B4

Chapter 13

1. *Studs Terkel's Working*, DVD, 1982, Broadway Theater Archive, Image Entertainment
2. "How One Black Woman Lands Her Jobs; Risks and Networking," *The Wall Street Journal*, March 4, 2003, page B1
3. Interview with Gay Vernon, WMJZ Radio, Boston, April 2002
4. "Revenge of the Retirees," *Business Week*, November 18, 2002, page 125
5. *Fortune*, March 3, 2003, page 150[A]

6. TED Conference, February 25 – March 3, 2003
7. *BusinessWoman* magazine, Fall 2002

Chapter 14

1. *Search for a Simpler Way*. For more, see Chapters 13 and 30

Chapter 16

1. *Search for a Simpler Way* findings, Top sources of work complexity:
   1) Lack of Integration of Change **2)** Unclear Goals and Objectives **3)** How We Communicate. For full study results, go to www.simplerwork.com

Chapter 17

1. *Search for a Simpler Way*, 1996 to 2003, based on over 230 interviews of those who identified successful strategies for dealing with managers who passed on too much

Chapter 18

1. *Search for a Simpler Way*, 1997 to 2003, over 400 interviews. While the exact percentage of teammates who have taken the path of least resistance will vary widely based on a number of factors, when we described the behaviors to interviews, most everyone (8 out of 10) described those behaviors as coming from their teammates as well as from themselves
2. ibid., survey of 108 people who our interviews identified as following this basic approach

Chapter 19

1. *Search for a Simpler Way*, 1997 to 2003, over 310 interviews with those who identified themselves as having a proactive approach to doing less and accomplishing more
2. ibid., comparison of success rates declared by those who had a proactive approach for doing less with more and 400 interviewees who described themselves as having only occasional successes in doing less

Chapter 20

1. *Search for a Simpler Way*. Between 1997 and 2003, during our interviews with several hundred individuals who proactively managed how their company and managers used their time, we found more than 130 who listed specific strategies for managing training efforts. The recommendations and success rates in this chapter come from those interviews

Chapter 21

1. See Chapter 16 footnote

Chapter 22

1. *Search for a Simpler Way* findings from more than 150 interviews about compensation, performance management, and performance appraisals, 1995 – 2003
2. *Harvard Business Review*, January 2003, "Management by Whose Objectives," by Harry Levinson, page 107

Chapter 23

1. *Search for a Simpler Way*, based on interviews of more than 100 people about successful budget request strategies

Chapter 24

1. "The Accidental CEO," *Fortune* Magazine, June 23, 2003, page 58

Chapter 29

1. "End of the Paper Chase," *Business 2.0*, March 2003, page 64
2. "Who's Minding the Store?" *Business 2.0*, February 2003, page 70
3. "An On-the-Job Hazard: The Corporate Travel Office," *Wall Street Journal*, June 25, 2003, page D1
4. ROI Institute, June 10, 2003 newsletter
5. "How Big Blue is Turning Geeks into Gold," *Fortune* magazine, June 9, 2003, page 140
6. "Tech Slowdown Lets Buyers Squeeze Suppliers," *Wall Street Journal*, March 11, 2003, page A6
7. "Money Men See Beauty in Human Capital," *Financial Times*, March 7, 2003, page VI.
   For more, go to www.mercerhr.com

Chapter 30

1. "Moving into the Future," *Newsweek*, April 19, 2002, page 40
2. *Fortune* magazine, March 18, 2002, page 184

Chapter 32

1. http://www.gallup.com/management/Q12_system.asp
2. *Work 2.0*, pages 50-52
3. *Fortune* magazine, October 28, 2002, page 137

Acknowledgments
Thanks!

These are the people who made sure I was true to myself....

Family. We've always blurred the line between life, work, and fun. (Until he was six, my son thought our office in Soho, New York, was just another place for birthday parties, scavenger hunts, and where his mom had a rooftop garden.) Thank you Louise and Ian for all your support, love, and laughter through crazy projects like this one.

My mom passed away in 1994, and my dad in 2000. I continue to be grateful to them that I was raised to follow my passions, dreams, creativity, and values.

•

And these are the people who made sure I stayed true to you....

Work-in-Progress Readers. Somebody had to tell Bill that his earliest drafts were incoherent babblings, and set him on the right path! These wonderful people provided that necessary service: Mary Ann Allison, Michael Ayers, Tami Belt, Dennis Bonilla, Carol Cole-Lewis, Ray Dempsey, Chris Ernst, Tom Farmer, Alden Globe, Erica Gold, Mike Grabowski, David Jardin, Craig Jennings, Ira Kasden, Mark Koskiniemi, Leslie Kossoff, Tom Kunz, Scott Leavitt, George Lixfield, Chris Macrae, Alicia Mandel, Tom Mott, Karen Perego, Jim Shanley, PJ Smoot, Beth Stoner, Stacey Wagoner, Mike Wittenstein. Thanks guys!

Book Teammates. I owe Nick Philipson, Elizabeth Carduff, and David Goehring soooooo much. They had the original faith in me that launched my first three books. Especially Nick, who took an editorial virgin and mentored me. Then the Perseus Books folks handed off to my new teammates at Basic Books. To my wonderful editor and new partner-in-crime, Bill Frucht, and Liz Maguire, Stephen Bottum, David Shoemaker, Will Morrison, and so many others...

Thank you for everything!

Before Bill Frucht saw them, every draft of every chapter would go to Lisa Adams, my agent. Each time, the draft would come back with 75 percent red "suggested" changes. If anything in this book is concise, compelling and clear, Lisa deserves the kudos. Wow... Lisa, you're the best!

Design and Production. With two kids crawling or crying nearby, and with the patience of a saint, my production buddy, Aimee Leary at Final Art, transformed my scribbles into wonderful page designs. Mark and Matt Versaggi worked tirelessly on the e-companion site, www.simplerwork.com. Marietta Urban oversaw pre-press production and printing. Rick Pracher created the wonderful cover that grabbed your attention and Merrill Gilfillan dotted every "i" in the proofing process. These are the talented people who turned my words into something useful, helpful, and eye-catching. I'm extremely grateful to each of you. Thanks!

Book Interviewees and Anonymous Contributors. I didn't really author this book. You did, or people who are just like you. Thousands of people who were either searching in the dark for shut-off valves, or who had flashlights, pointing the way. This is their book, their story, and your book, your story.

Also: scores of people (whose names you see in the index) generously answered my phone calls and emails, and let me bug them in person for their stories. Finally, a couple hundred panelists tried and critiqued every to-do in this book. They asked to remain anonymous because they didn't want their bosses to know about their passion for doing less and their talent in creating workarounds. My thanks to each of you!

My inspiration. You! Thank you.

Subject Index

Subject Index

Subject Index

Subject Index

People Index